Dear Amy & Eric,

We are sharing this & one with each of our grandchildren this Christmas in lieu of "Socks". We know the author, Keith Tyner.

Keith wrote from his heart and as a Financial Advisor taking the material for his book from his personal experiences and those of his clients. He is our Financial Advisor and our friend. We hope you view this book as positive. We wish you a most joyful Christmas!

Love Continuously,
Grandpa & Grandma
Gallaway

Financial Survivors

A Guide for Living Before Loss

Financial Survivors

A Guide for
Living Before Loss

Keith A. Tyner, CFP

PUBLISHING

Dallas, Texas

This publication is designed to provide general information. Because individual legal, tax, and financial situations are different, readers should seek specific advice. For this reason, the reader is advised to consult with his or her own attorney, accountant, and/or other advisor regarding the individual's specific situation. The author has taken reasonable precautions in the preparation of this book and believes that the information presented in the book is accurate as of the date it was written. However, neither the author nor publisher assumes any responsibility for any errors or omissions. The author and publisher specifically disclaim any liability resulting from the use or application of the information contained in this book, and the information is not intended to serve as legal, tax, or other financial advice related to individual situations. Examples are for informational purposes only and may not be representative of the experiences of other clients. Illustrations are hypothetical and are not intended to represent or project actual performance or results.

First printing 2008

ISBN 978-0-9796068-2-3

LCCN 2007927488

ATTENTION CORPORATIONS, UNIVERSITIES, COLLEGES, AND PRO-FESSIONAL ORGANIZATIONS: Quantity discounts are available on bulk purchases of this book for educational use, gift purposes, or as premiums for increasing magazine subscriptions or renewals. Special books or book excerpts can also be created to fit specific needs. For information, please contact CEO IQ Publishing, 2625 Main Street, Dallas, TX 75226, (214) 752-3647.

Table of Contents

Introduction

The catalyst to pen this book was not the reality of death, but the anxiety I noticed among my clients' survivors in their efforts to sort through the affairs of a loved one. Initially, I began writing notes to the survivors, when I would learn of the passing, encouraging them to take a breather and then call me in two to three weeks, granting them priority in my meeting schedule.

Over time, I was writing more and more notes of that type and frequently answering similar questions. An idea grew: provide clients and their families with a guide to help them tend to the affairs of their loved ones. As I began writing the first few chapters I found that I was writing more or less from the survivor's point of view. After a few clients had read rough drafts, the most common suggestion was that this should be a book that—far and away—helps people most when read *long before* a death occurs. But whose death? Sometimes the death being prepared for in advance is someone else's death, for example, the death of a loved one such as your spouse or parent or grandparent. You and this loved one are making provisions in advance for the survivors. Sometimes the death being prepared for is your own: you want to simplify for family members the process to deal with finances and a host of other matters once you are gone.

Obituaries call family members left behind after the death of a loved one "survivors." By making plans in advance, you can diminish the stress on your survivors while providing financially for them as well. Many people not only find it difficult to "survive" a loved one's death and to deal with the grief, but also they find it overwhelming to tend to financial situations. Planning in advance is for *them*, for your survivors; taking action on these plans will ensure they *survive*. This book is designed to guide you and your loved ones through the planning process and to make it easy to execute the steps in the plan. It can be used as a reference to zero-in on a decision about specific life matters. The book is formatted to allow room in the margins to make notes, and for those who don't need all the details, it is streamlined with topic summaries, to-do lists, and references to sources within the text.

Because this book is written as both a proactive and reactive document, most of the suggestions pertain to preventive actions, but some pertain to actions taken by the survivors after the fact. It is also ordered in a proactive fashion, however if you are reading from a reactive vantage point, you may consider starting with Chapter 8 and working your way backward.

As you use this guide, consider it a preemptive planner that will enable you to *live life with no regrets by taking action before a loss*. Our lives are but a flash in time. Call your special loved ones today; tell them exactly how you feel about them! Demonstrate how much you love them by using this guide to prepare them to not only survive a passing but also to live with abundance beyond it.

Chapter 1

Anticipating a Different Future

Whether you are reading this in a proactive fashion or you are trying to pick up the pieces after the loss of a loved one, many of the decisions discussed in this guide are subjective and unique to each family. However, the topics were specifically selected because they are common issues many of us need to address. This guide is intended to help you, and those you love, to anticipate and act today regarding the inevitable changes that will accompany loss sometime in the future.

Grieving affects us all differently. Some people can cycle through grief in a matter of months; others require years. There is no way to replace your loved ones. Precious memories of your time together are priceless. But the rhythm of the financial world beats more like a gong than a heartbeat. The necessary interactions with the gong can be cold and impersonal. You can take a little of the chill from these issues by acting today at a measured pace.

In reality, proceeding at a slow, methodical pace enables you to successfully achieve closure with the gong-sounding issues and in a manner that helps you stay in touch with your own heartbeat as you process the thoughts and intentions of your loved ones. You *can* complete the necessary administrative issues in a timely manner.

Write your loved ones a love note today.

Special Assignment: As you read this, record your thoughts in the margin about areas that strike a chord with you. Those notes might allow your loved ones who may one day survive you to have more clarity when the need arises to actually respond to your life and death. You can even take this effort to the next level. Use this chapter as a catalyst to list the individuals you believe would need to read this book as it relates to your life. Then write each one a final love note. Tell each why he or she is so special in your eyes, relate the most memorable times you shared, and confess any regrets you have in regard to your relationship. Express how precious your love is for each one of them. Include any other cherished thought you would like to leave with them, anything you want to be certain they know. Omit negative comments in these love letters. Attach a copy of this book with your notes inside.

After you have written these letters, take time to reread them to make sure you have completely disclosed how you feel about the recipients in your heart. What better inheritance could your loved ones ever receive from you than to know how dear they are to you in a clear and concise letter and to also offer the opportunity to express their thoughts to you?

No doubt you may have done this exercise many times in the past. Many of the recommendations in this book offer practical solutions to practical issues of life. But the conclusion of this subject is that life is impractical. Or perhaps I should say life is *more than* practical. It transcends the practical realm. Life is about relationships—our relationship with God, our relationships with family, and our relationships with our friends.

Many of us may take time to clean up the practical matters before our life comes to a close. These are the things that bang like a gong. They are important, but the things that are connected to the heartbeat of life are more important. Take time now to clarify and communicate the issues dearest to you. If there are relationships that are strained, be a peacemaker. If there are uplifting words that need to be spoken, say them. If there are gifts that need to be given, give them.

If you are reading this, you have the choice to live your life without regrets. Take the necessary steps today to do so. Life is short, and its pace accelerates. This is the day to do the things your *heart* is crying out for you to complete.

Planning Guide for Your Loved Ones

Location of Important Documents

Indicate one of these choices or a *specific alternative.*

- Exact location at home
- Exact location at work
- Safe deposit box
- Attorney's office

Cemetery Arrangement Documents

_____

Funeral Arrangement Documents

_____

Will(s) / Trust(s)

_____

Birth Certificate(s)

_____

Marriage License

_____

Citizenship Papers

_____

Veteran's Discharge Certificate(s)

_____

Social Security Card(s)

_____

Life Insurance Policies

_____

Health and Disability Policies

_____

Home/Auto Policies

_____

Auto Titles

_____

Mortgages/Loans Documents

_____

Real Estate Deeds

_____

Bank Statements

_____

Stock/Bond Certificates

_____

Documents that will be needed immediately should not be stored in a safe deposit box.

Pension/IRA Information

_____

Income Tax Returns

_____

Safe Deposit Box Key

_____

Passwords/User IDs/Combinations

_____

It's All About You

My immediate family includes seven people. Connie and I constantly balance our priorities. Occasionally there is a disagreement about our choices and a discussion evolves. When I am being questioned about our prioritization efforts, I frequently point out to my offspring, "It's not *all* about you!" This statement doesn't create a lot of agreement.

But to survivors, I change my mantra to, "It *is* all about you!" Your survivors need to take care of themselves and look at life from a slightly different perspective prior to their loss. Their physical, fiscal, and social well-being are important and may benefit from some practical insight.

A Healthy Future

Your death or disability can have adverse effects on your loved ones' health. Death is such a difficult reality to endure physically, mentally, emotionally, and spiritually; it is easy for the survivors to ignore their own health. *Their health is a priority over other considerations. Encourage them to take care of themselves.*

As your health begins to deteriorate, it can adversely affect your caregivers and other loved ones. Encourage them to pay close attention to their own health.

When my father's health began to deteriorate, it had a negative effect on my mother and my sister. Both battled with the influence of increased stress in their lives. Ultimately, it caused my mother to be hospitalized with heart problems.

Encouraging your loved ones to consider and manage their own health may also require the assistance of a trustworthy outsider to provide an extra set of ears and possibly the attention of an extra set

Take care of yourself.

of eyes. Suggest that they get a physical and let their doctor know about their increased stress. Awareness of possible physical ailments beforehand will make them easier to recognize should they manifest later. Their doctor has likely helped other patients manage their health during a period of grief and can offer some practical suggestions and insight, as well as any necessary medical treatments for conditions that might enable you or a loved one cope better after a future loss. If you have already suffered a loss, the extra set of ears will ensure your doctor is aware of the dramatic change in your life and can help you process his or her suggestions.

The necessity of an extra set of eyes is to have someone close to you visibly note and help you and your loved ones to respond to any drastic physical changes that might be indicators of other problems you may not notice due to their gradual evolution. Allowing someone you love and trust the freedom to point out any noticeable changes might help save you from more drastic problems that could unfold.

Don't ignore symptoms of depression.

Something else to anticipate is the idea of entropy, the process of running down or a measure of random errors or disorder that occurs within a system or situation. This principle is also true with regard to our bodies. This phenomenon became clear to me when I was in my twenties as my bangs gradually worked their way to the back of my head.

However, there are temporary disruptions to our bodies that can become more permanent and more dangerous without attention. A common example for many people is depression. Depression is typical affliction that affects people who are grieving, and yet this ailment can become progressively more dangerous without attention. Depression is like carbon monoxide poisoning; there is no smell or alarm that sounds to alert its presence and undetected it can be very hazardous. Discuss your feelings with your friends and family.

Tip: Use online tools, such as the following Web site, to help determine if you or someone you love is suffering from depression:

www.maayoclinic.com/health/drepression/MH00103_D

Depression attacked me in the past. Some common symptoms are loss of energy, loss of hunger, loss of enthusiasm, and a pessimistic view of the future. The cure may be as simple as a caring friend encouraging you through the time of disappointment, or it may be more complicated and require medical assistance. Depression needs to be brought to the attention of someone who can help you as soon as possible.

> *Here are some essential ideas that pertain to your health to consider before a death in your family becomes imminent (due a chronic illness or old age):*
>
> - Get plenty of sleep at a normal time and duration.
> - Exercise four or five times weekly, even if it is simply a walk around your neighborhood.
> - Eat regularly and monitor your weight for any changes.
> - Visit your doctor annually.
> - Make sure you are connected socially:
>   Join a church.
>   Join a club.
>   Get involved in a neighborhood group.
>   Join a grief support group.
> - Get outside and enjoy plenty of sunshine.

Some of these ideas may seem trivial, but you may require some initiative to start. Hopefully you have a friend in whom you can confide who can help you pay attention to these areas.

Preventative Maintenance

Whether you call it entropy, gravity, or the aging process, there is the chance that all of us will struggle with health issues at some point in life. Some of the ideas above may delay or help minimize the effects of illness. However, there are some practical steps you can take to minimize the complexity of managing a loved one's illness.

Open Communication

An interesting statistic in the financial planning process is how few families have wills or estate plans in place. According to an article in

Let your loved ones know your health-care wishes while you are healthy.

the *Wall Street Journal* posted on Lawyers.com, fewer than 42 percent of adults have wills.[1] People do not like to talk about death or dying. Although there is a 100 percent chance we will all experience both death and dying, something inside us wants to avoid the conversation at all costs.

Discuss, in advance, your thoughts with your loved ones about your health. Such discussions are often like the proverbially huge elephant in the middle of the room. Everyone sees it, but no one wants to discuss it. Let your family know your thoughts.

My father's health began a rapid decline during his final years. Although his health was getting progressively worse, none of his ailments were fatal. As a result, no one wanted to suggest to him that he and my mother could no longer live on their own. Sixty days before his last Thanksgiving, his pastor called me and said, "Keith, you need to kick your parents out of their house!" He recognized that their health needs were becoming urgent and that living alone was no longer a good option. You can imagine the horror I felt as I contemplated trying to have a conversation on that subject with my parents. Although I did not like the message, their pastor was telling the truth.

The messenger in this situation was actually our extra set of eyes. The pastor was able to objectively see the situation and unemotionally give counsel. This was one of the most difficult mind games of my life, trying to motivate myself to have this conversation with my parents.

If only Mom and Dad were counseled earlier to offer us the freedom to *tell them* if and when we felt it was becoming apparent that changes needed to be made! The bridge to that conversation might still have been difficult, but it would have been somewhat easier.

There are several things you should consider communicating to your future decision makers. And if open communication is a difficult endeavor for you, you might consider someone mediating this initial discussion to set the dialogue in motion. My parents' pastor offered to fill that role when my parents needed to hear that their health needs had grown to a point that no longer allowed my parents to adequately take care of themselves and that they needed us to help them make important decisions.

[1] Kathy Chu, "Fewer Estates Exercise Will Power," *Wall Street Journal*, June 10, 2004, Lawyers.com, www.lawyers.com/pdc/pressroom/article_wsj061004.asp (accessed May 25, 2007).

Here's another example: You might be able to unemotionally discuss some thoughts with your financial consultant but not with your children. In this case, try to schedule a meeting at your financial consultant's office with your children and have the consultant initiate the conversation and provide an objective outsider's perspective.

The importance of discussing health issues *prior to* an illness is significant. When you are reasonably healthy, discussing a hypothetical future illness is less emotional and less threatening than discussing an actual ailment. During an illness, emotions are generally supercharged and the individuals who are sick find the discussions more taxing.

Take the time now to determine who will be acting as your health-care power of attorney to clearly convey your desires regarding a prolonged illness. You might help him or her understand the thought process involved in creating your living will if you have such a document.

You might also address how much time your caregiver would spend away from his or her healthy family members while caring for you during your illness. *Guilt is a challenge for your caregivers, and during an illness it might be difficult for them to make appropriate allocations of their own time.* There are other topics you can discuss in these conversations, including the housing alternatives, which are addressed later in this book.

Continued health is always uncertain. There are preventative maintenance issues you can address, but some things can flare up without warning. Don't be afraid to tell your loved ones your thoughts. They will be grateful and it will improve everyone's peace of mind!

Socially Speaking

The loss of a special person can leave an emotional void. When you lose a spouse, you may be vulnerable for a long time. Some people choose to never marry again and others have no clear direction in that regard.

In 1988, my sister-in-law was tragically killed by a drunk driver. Her widower, father of four youngsters, was hospitalized for several weeks due to the accident. The loss he felt was not only emotional but also practical, as he considered the responsibility of taking care of four children on his own. It was impossible to predict what would happen in his life at that point in time, but it was clear he would have difficult days ahead.

Not too many months after his accident, he was introduced to a beautiful young lady who wanted to marry someone in the ministry. It seemed like a miraculous pairing of people, but the complexity of the situation required some sensitive efforts. It was amazing to watch how the family welcomed his new bride into the fold.

Dating Again

There is no set standard regarding how long an individual should wait after being widowed before beginning to date again. But the very first date can cause conflict within the family arising from parents, children, and siblings of the deceased. It can be an awkward time for everyone involved.

Open communication about the initiation of dating can make the transition more palatable for all. There is something about dating again that emphasizes the finality of a loved one's death. It can stir up many of the emotions that were initially generated and can cause people to act and say things they might not otherwise do or say.

It makes sense to bridge conversations of this type before there are any dating relationships underway. Before an actual, specific person enters the picture, the discussion can be more hypothetical and less emotional, and this is definitely a plus. The inclusion of a specific person in the discussion complicates the topic, changing it from a conceptual idea to a perceived attack against the new sweetheart.

Whichever side of the discussion you find yourself on, slow down long enough to consider the other person's point of view. As you discuss the possibilities of the future, be patient with others. It is probable that everyone involved is still dealing with some level of grief.

Dating may result in a trip down the aisle. In addition to all the other important considerations, this idea also has financial implications that can affect many of the survivors. The survivor's nest egg may be at risk in the event of another marriage, and adult children are often concerned about both their parent's well-being as well as the possibility that their potential inheritance may be jeopardized.

Such fears may never be vocalized, but they're a reality of the world in which we live. Hopefully the widow(er) is primarily motivated by love for the new significant other, but financial concerns about the future can also figure in. Although money should not be the decisive element in a marriage situation, it can be more complicated in a second marriage.

This is a discussion that is better served if it happens prior to including a personality in the mix. It is worthwhile to bridge a conversation with your family about the idea of dating again and the implications. This might be an awkward discussion, but the involvement of a mediator, such as a pastor or friend, may help develop a productive conversation.

Legally Speaking

There is something about the statement, "Honey, I think we need prenuptial agreements" that tends to strip away the romance of the moment. Such a conversation could bring an otherwise successful relationship to a screeching halt. So what can people do about the financial components when considering remarriage?

A prenuptial agreement is a legal document that describes the distribution of financial assets upon the dissolution of a marriage. It specifically defines where assets will be distributed. Often it specifies that a person's children, rather than the new spouse, will become that person's beneficiaries in the event of death. It is often seen as a way to protect children from a surviving stepparent who might be inclined to hoard an inheritance or to inequitably distribute the inheritance.

> **Source:** There are numerous Web sites that offer practical advice about the sensitive issues surrounding remarriage. One helpful site is: www.howtoremarry.com.

We live in an imperfect world and there are people who prey on others simply to seize some of their financial wealth (such as a second husband or wife who would selfishly not provide for stepchildren in

Are you familiar with prenuptial agreements?

Financial concerns of a new marriage can be addressed creatively.

the event of the spouse's death). I advise seeking professional counsel and moving slowly into new relationships.

Prenuptial agreements are necessary to consider before you begin dating again. Whether or not they are the right solution for your situation is completely subjective. But to ignore the issue and hope that your situation will all work out for the best is often a naïve idea. Thinking about, deciding about, and communicating about prenuptials *before* you start dating is wisest. You don't want to grow close to someone and only then find out that the two of you have very different ideas regarding prenuptials. If you do, you will likely either end the relationship sadly, or one person will reluctantly give in to the other's wishes. Neither choice is a desirable or very healthy option.

If you are interested in a prenuptial agreement, the conversation with your significant other should prove interesting. I believe the discussion of such a document must begin very early in a relationship and not the week before the wedding. Many states have time parameters established concerning how soon before a wedding that prenuptial documents must be signed.

As you consider the future, both your physical and social health revolves around your particular choices. Make sure you are comfortable with the variables and move forward as your heart leads. When in doubt, be sure to discuss your thoughts, fears, concerns, and intentions with your loved ones. Communication is critical to minimizing conflict.

Stuff, Stuff, and More Stuff

George Carlin's old comedy routine tells the story about "stuff." Carlin suggests we spend our lives buying, storing, moving, cleaning, maintaining, and protecting our stuff. We even have suitcases so we can pack a subset of our stuff and take it with us on trips.

It is amazing how quickly stuff accumulates. Even more amazing is how little of it we actually use in any given day. A common pack rat mantra is: "I can't get rid of any of my stuff because I might need it one day." It seems the impoverished nature of the Great Depression era helped escalate this mindset with folks who survived it.

Generally, the more stuff you have, the less time and money you have for God, your family, your friends, and yourself. So, do you own your stuff or does it own you? Belongings have a way of consuming our time and energy.

Unfortunately, possessions can sometimes cause conflict among family members after the loss of a loved one. My grandmother had a breakfast specialty that my two siblings and I longed for every time we visited her—square eggs. She had a pan that poached four square eggs at once. When she passed away, all three of us separately bugged my uncle for the pan. We all had sentimental ties to having breakfast with Grandma and that pan seemed to tie the memories back to her.

Recently, Uncle Bill gave the pan to my older brother Randy. I cannot speak for my sister, but I know the instant the gift was given away, something in me was envious of Randy. It could have been easy to grow angry about something as silly as a pan used to make square eggs. Thankfully I have seen the danger of assigning too much value to stuff, and I got over my envy quickly.

> Your stuff does not define who you are, but it can own you if you let it.

> Avoid attaching sentimental value to all of your loved one's assets.

Creative
solutions for
dividing
possessions
can keep
peace in the
family.

There is no way to know for sure how your loved ones will be affected by your possessions. Consequently, it is better if you act in advance to help minimize the possibility of conflict: encourage your heirs to let you know which possessions they have strong ties to.

Relationships with family members may be lost or damaged simply because people care too much about who gets what. This is probably the last thing you want to happen as a result of the things you acquire during your lifetime. So, as much as possible, help your heirs let those things go.

When I have inherited belongings from my ancestors, I have tried to find small possessions with big meaning. This effort allows me the opportunity to have a keepsake without having to build a storage barn in which to store it.

What Property Should Go Where?

Because belongings, and divvying them up, can be controversial, it is worth considering in advance some ways to minimize the strife and hurt feelings before they become a wedge in family relationships. Estate planning attorneys are familiar with the pitfalls of "stuff." If you sense that dividing up the stuff is a potential problem within your family, be sure to point it out to your attorney so he or she can include some ideas in your estate plan to proactively address the issue.

Creative Solutions:

- Have a Sticker Party with your heirs. Each heir receives ten stickers of a particular color. The heirs take turns placing stickers on pieces of stuff until their stickers are gone. Depending on the number of heirs, a good amount of your stuff could be designated in advance for beneficiary purposes. To make the party more enjoyable, have each person discuss why he or she selected each object.
- Give your loved ones gifts from your possessions each time they visit. As a result, there is less and less stuff left to fuss over at a later date.

- Use a deadline approach. Provide a clause in your will dictating all heirs to settle on the distribution of the stuff by a specific deadline. If they cannot come to agreement by that deadline, then charity gets it all or it is put up for auction!
- Consider an auction. Place all of the property up for auction and your heirs can bid on the items they want. The proceeds can then be split among them according to your estate documents.

Sorting Through Belongings

Choosing to thin out your belongings during your lifetime can minimize the amount of effort your loved ones will need to exert at a later date and can also help you financially. It is said, "One man's trash is another man's treasure." Clearly, sorting through a loved one's stuff brings this maxim to life. Even sorting through your own property can be a sentimental journey. But don't let sentiment override the reality that people tend to keep unnecessary artifacts. Your loved ones may need to acquire a larger house if they were to keep all of your stuff! Try sorting stuff into distinct categories: keepers, charitable gifts, items for auction, and trash.

Keepers are things of value that are also functional for your particular situation. But beware: things we want to call "keepers" are more often actually better candidates for "charitable gifts." How about a screwdriver? Do you own one, two, or three? If your children were to inherit ten more would they classify them as keepers or charitable gifts? It is completely subjective, but few people really need more than three or four screwdrivers.

A solution might be keeping the screwdrivers you frequently use and donating the other ones to charity. The magnitude of your keeper pile will correlate closely with the size of the "pack rat" gene you inherited.

Charitable gifts are a nice alternative to keeping more possessions than you need. There are scores of less fortunate people, and choosing to donate effects will bless their lives. It is a neat idea that your stuff can bless others! There are a variety of charities to consider as recipients of your property.

Sort belongings into four categories:

1) keepers
2) charitable gifts
3) auction assets
4) trash

There are tax advantages to gifting to charity, and some recordkeeping ideas are suggested below. But keep in mind your charitable gifts do not have to go to tax-deductible charities. Who knows? There may be younger family members who would benefit greatly from some screwdrivers, spatulas, or spoon collections. Don't rule out the possibility that non-heir family members or friends might also benefit from your stuff.

> **Source:** If you want your material items to go to a charity, work with family members in advance to choose one that brings added meaning to your legacy.

Tip:
A good resource for finding a charity is:

www.charitynavigator.org

Auction assets can range from the obscure to the valuable. Auctions have been transformed by the Internet. You may have local auction companies coordinate the sale of these items or you might choose to go high tech and use a service like eBay. Today there are even local eBay retailers who will sell your property for you.

Tip:
You can find an eBay store near you by going to:

www.ebaydropoffsites.net

Regardless of the arena you choose, make sure you understand the costs associated with auctioning goods. If you are auctioning antiques and valuables that you are unfamiliar with, secure the advice of experts who can help you understand the value of the assets. A benefit of using local auction companies is that they will often come to your house, peruse the goods that are up for auction, and give you an idea about their marketability.

During my father's latter years, he wanted a new computer but was not interested in cashing in investments to fund the model he wanted.

He opted to auction some of his pens and marbles he had collected in recent years. To my utter surprise, the marbles and pens netted nearly $10,000. Your belongings from a former day could help fund your current day's desires.

Trash would seem to be a straightforward selection, but the "one man's trash" phenomenon can make this a complicated effort. One of my clients went through the sorting process and had all four piles segregated from his parents' house. Intuitively, the keeper pile would hold the greatest value, followed by the auction stuff, charitable gifts, and finally the trash. But when his brother surveyed the sorting process, he immediately migrated to the bags of trash. My client was amazed by his brother's attraction to the items in the junk pile.

Let your personal representative know how controversial this component of being a survivor can be. Let your loved ones know your ideas concerning how to resolve any conflicts and encourage them to realize there is no way of understanding another person's ability to attach sentimental value to things. Allow people room to express themselves, and if they need to sift through the trash pile, let them do what they need to do.

Normally clothing is not the stuff that causes division among the heirs. But clothes could be underappreciated in their charitable value. Take some time to make sure you make the most of your clothes.

What about All These Clothes?

That special sweater, red dress, and even the winter coat you used to wear were all nice during their time. But if you are not wearing them anymore, now is the time to give them away, and you must address the lingering question about how to properly distribute them.

There may be family members or friends who would benefit from acquiring some of your wardrobe. But possibly there are clothes you no longer need that may bring substantial financial benefits to you by carefully inventorying them and then gifting them to an appropriate charity.

Inventorying the clothing might seem tedious and a bit of an over-kill, but if you think about it, there is often great value in one's wardrobe. A pair of dress shoes can easily approach $100 or more,

> If you are the personal representative, be aware of emotions belongings can evoke.

and tennis shoes are often in the same price range. Suits and dress clothes can also tally up pretty quickly. If your loved one had an extensive wardrobe, there could be substantial value in just one closet.

Don't underestimate the charitable value of clothes.

To inventory clothes, you might make a list of types of clothing along with a rating system of the condition (i.e., new, good, or poor). This inventory will be important as you assess a value for your income taxes.

If you itemize your deductions for your taxes, the gift of these clothes to a charity can be included as a non-cash charitable donation. If the value of all of your non-cash contributions in a year exceeds $500, your accountant will need to complete form 8283 to deduct the value from your taxes.

Non-cash charitable gifts can be tax deductible.

If the clothes were your spouse's, you might want to ask your tax advisor whether it is more beneficial to give them away in the current tax year or wait for a future year. Widows and widowers are allowed to continue filing their taxes as married for the year their spouse dies.

Source: Your tax advisor should be able to give you an idea when the deduction would be most suitable for your situation. There is a handy resource available called *It's Deductible: The Blue Book for Donated Items*, which provides values for a variety of different assets, including clothes, that you can use to write off of your income taxes. Intuit, the source of Quicken, QuickBooks, and TurboTax, is the provider of this resource. It is available in software form online and can be an easy solution for inventorying your gifts.

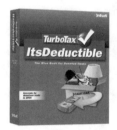

You can purchase this tool at: www.intuit.com.

Although this topic seems a bit distasteful, it is important to manage your resources as wisely as possible. If you simply give the articles to charity and assume a random blanket value, you could be giving thousands of dollars away to Uncle Sam. Take the time to carefully go through the items you intend to give to charity and make an inventory.

Keep a receipt from the charity for your tax records to verify the contribution. It is not the charity's responsibility to value the articles;

that is why *It's Deductible* is a good tool. If this process is too over-whelming, check with a sibling, child, or friend to see if one of them is willing to help you with this endeavor.

It is worthwhile to repeat this effort every year. You may want to clean out your closet in a manner that segregates clothes you use frequently from those you seldom use. A coat of dust across the top of your not-so-frequently-used items indicates they may be good candidates to give away the next time you make a charitable contribution.

Anticipating Strategic Changes

Change is difficult even in the best of times. Unfortunately, the loss of a loved one may precipitate changes you have not considered. Preparing in advance for life's tragedies helps diminish some of the negative impact they have on life.

For example, you should anticipate adjustments in your investments, income, spending, housing, taxes, and other areas. Whether these changes are actually initiated may be at your discretion. The changes necessary may be difficult to actually implement. These changes are often accompanied by sentimental thoughts and fears, even uncertainty. They will probably be best processed with the involvement of your extra set of ears.

Indecision is a bad decision. It might seem easier not to make necessary decisions, but all postponing generally does is to prolong a difficult decision to a time that might be even more complex. For example, if you need to move from a large house to something smaller, ignoring the decision will not negate the reality that you are in the wrong place.

Inherited assets are your assets.

The next few pages address some areas of possible change in a candid format. They are not intended to be discourteous but are meant to point out some common pitfalls and offer some general ideas.

Cleaning Up Your *Investments*

Did you notice the pronoun in the headline? Your investments are yours as long as you are living. As rhetorical as this might seem it is an important point to consider. Normally your heirs will have little knowledge of the reasoning behind the different investments you own. And yet sometimes they may assume you would want them to hold the investments you bought indefinitely.

Point out to your heirs that, as the survivors and the beneficiaries, your investments have now become theirs and they need to manage them wisely to meet their needs.

I remember my grandmother telling me nearly twenty years after Grandpa's death how she had not touched any of "his" money. I did not have the heart to tell her that his contractual rights to the investments had ceased.

There seems to be an emotional tie to the resources left by the deceased. Often those resources are somehow segregated and considered different from other assets available to the survivor. This approach can be bad for your survivors' financial health. Investments are dynamic entities. They generally have finite lifetimes and are oblivious to the personalities of the individuals who own them. There is no assurance an inherited investment will be a good investment the day it is inherited, let alone twenty years later. Quite frankly, it might not have been a good one the day you made it.

Encourage your heirs to avoid the temptation of attaching sentimental value to investments. Investments are designed to help the owner grow wealth. Individual stocks have a tendency to evoke more sentimental ties than other investments. Stocks are risky. Your children blindly holding onto a stock because you left it to them may result in their wealth being diminished.

> **Case in Point:** A utility company in a large metropolitan city lost 90 percent of its former value in the first few years of the new millennium. A large pharmaceutical company lost 50 percent of its value. Some five years later, as I write this chapter, neither has recovered. Today it appears the pharmaceutical industry may be in a slow growth mode for several years to come. Suppose you retired from a pharmaceutical company and much of your wealth is attached to its stock. Your children may be slow to sell it and the capital could sit idly for the foreseeable future.

Investments change and often have finite lifetimes.

Investments should not have sentimental value, only market value.

Indecision is a bad decision.

Investment: Proactive Action Plan

If you are cleaning up a portfolio of investments or you are assisting an ailing loved one to do so, consider the following:

- It's a good idea to have a professional help you review the portfolio as if you were going to invest cash in the current marketplace. If the existing investment isn't one in which new capital would be added, it makes sense to sell it and prepare to reinvest elsewhere, particularly if there are multiple beneficiaries.
- Cash is generally the easiest asset to distribute to beneficiaries.
- In the process of cleaning up one's investments, it may simplify things to establish an estate or trust account at one financial institution and organize the financial assets in a central location. The more accounts there are, the more time consuming this endeavor may be. A financial advisor should be helpful in the consolidation effort.
- Deal with the DRIPs, an acronym for investment accounts called "dividend reinvestment plans." Have you heard of the Chinese water torture? It is the process of tying someone down and then letting water slowly drip on that person. Theoretically the dripping process would drive the victim insane. This investment vehicle can similarly drip on you and cause additional stress, perhaps even make you feel as if you were being driven insane. Many Fortune 500 companies that pay dividends have these investment accounts available to their shareholders. DRIPs usually offer an efficient way to compound dividends, but they can cause a tortuous ordeal for survivors. Frequently, the trustee of these accounts is a highly automated company with Internet sites or recorded lines on their toll-free number. It can be extremely difficult to reach a live service representative.

Have a professional review the investments you inherit.

Dividend reinvestment plans are difficult to manage for many people.

The effort to reregister securities through dividend reinvestment plans (DRIPs) can be somewhat regimented and often difficult. *It's a good idea to minimize the use of DRIPs if you are interested in simpli-*

Don't
handcuff
your heirs
with your
investment
philosophy.

fying your finances. Today most brokerage companies allow you to reinvest your dividends within a single account and do not require multiple third parties, 1099s, or toll-free numbers.

A short time ago a survivor called me with regard to a situation in which she inherited more than twenty separate dividend reinvestment plans. The process of cleaning up these accounts alone took many hours. If you are presented with such a situation, determine the trustee of the accounts and whether several are at the same organization. If the accounts are with the same trustee, work through the phone maze to talk with a supervisor. It is possible that a supervisor can coordinate an efficient transfer of the entire portfolio at the organization.

Tip: Computershare Investor Services, one of the largest DRIPs agents, allows you to access all of the accounts held by the company if you provide a social security number.

You can honor your loved ones by wisely managing your assets. Simplifying your holdings and consolidating your accounts is a wise course of action. Don't handcuff them with investments you bought in the past.

Tax Planning May Save You

Tax laws complicate life for most everyone. Although you may plan to leave your loved ones a nest egg to help finance their future, it might be unnecessarily reduced by taxes if you are not familiar with the rules or coached by someone who is. Two components of taxation to consider are whether any death taxes are possible and how to minimize the impact of income taxes.

Taxes are the tail and not the head of the decision process, and yet it is important to consider both components before you act. For example, today's tax law allows widows and widowers to file joint tax returns the year their spouse passes away. This information may help minimize the impact of taxes as you begin planning for the future.

A good accountant will help you consider the tax implications. Most accountants charge hourly rates for their services and starting rates average $75 per hour. This may be a sticker shock to some, but the amount a good accountant may save you in unnecessary taxes and frustration should exceed the amount of the fees.

A challenge in this regard might be finding an accountant who takes a proactive role in tax planning. Many accountants are more task-oriented and offer input only after you have questioned a particular issue. Ideally you will find an accountant who is abreast of the current tax laws and is willing to offer you unsolicited suggestions.

If you do not already have an established relationship with an accountant, you should be able to get a reliable referral from your financial consultant. Many financial consultants work hand-in-hand with accountants and are familiar with their skills and personality to the point that they can help you find someone right for your situation.

Your financial consultant can meet with your accountant to help clarify confusing situations and ask questions for you. This synergy between your accountant and financial consultant should help you make better decisions by leveraging current tax laws.

If you have attained age fifty-nine and a half it may be wise to close out employer retirement plans. Don't be in a hurry just because someone wants you to complete the paperwork. Be sure you have an extra set of ears along to help you to understand the options available. Employers normally provide a document entitled *Important Tax Information* to help you understand your options. You need to verify that you have read and that you understand this document before the process can proceed. If you are in a hurry, you might be tempted to acknowledge your understanding of the tax implications even if they are not clear to you. Take your time.

The Social Security Maze

Social Security was established in 1935 to provide retirement benefits for the aged. Through the years it has evolved to a more complex and widely encompassing social provision. The benefits vary broadly.

Usually with a death, the funeral home will issue death information directly to Social Security. Although the funeral home might provide this service, it is the responsibility of the family of the deceased to notify the Social Security Administration.

Don't make financial decisions solely on the tax implications.

Journal conversations with the Social Security Administration.

The comments in this section are intended to provide an on-ramp of education to prepare you to talk with a Social Security representative but not to engage in a comprehensive discussion. After completing this chapter, you will have a better understanding of the benefits available through Social Security and the methods of communication with the Social Security Administration.

Tip: The Social Security Administration (SSA) is available to help you and can be reached by phone at 1-800-772-1213. A representative can help you locate a local office and schedule an appointment. You might also read and/or download the SSA electronic publication *Social Security— Survivor Benefits*. You can access this e-book and other helpful information at *www.ssa.gov*. Talk to friends who have worked with SSA for more ideas.

Some of the benefits available to survivors include widow(er), widow(er) with children, and disabled survivor. The dollar amounts of the benefits vary. According to the SSA Web site, the average monthly benefit in 2006 was $1,008 for a widow(er), $2,167 for a widow(er) with two children, and $979 for disabled workers. These numbers do not indicate what you might receive but are listed to illustrate the wide-ranging benefits available.

Survivor benefits are available to a spouse and other family members.

Benefits to Consider:

What You Should Know Now

- The basic *death benefit* of $255 is payable to a spouse living with the deceased at the time of death or a child who would qualify for Social Security benefits based on the deceased's work record. If no spouse or child qualifies, this benefit will not be paid.
- *Survivor benefits* are available to a widow(er) as early as age sixty with reduced benefits. Additionally, a disabled widow(er) may receive benefits as early as age fifty.

  A widow(er) will receive benefits at any age if he or she cares for the deceased's child under age sixteen or if the child is disabled and receives Social Security benefits.

- Unmarried children under age eighteen, or up to age nineteen if they are attending school full time, are also eligible for benefits. The child can receive benefits at any age if the child was disabled prior to age twenty-two and remains disabled. Additionally, some stepchildren, grandchildren, or adopted children may qualify for survivor benefits. Dependent parents age sixty-two or older qualify for survivor benefits as well.
- A former spouse might qualify for the same benefits as a widow(er) if he or she was married to the deceased for at least ten years. Also, people collecting a widow(er)'s benefit can switch to their own benefit as early as age sixty-two. Often a survivor can collect one benefit at a reduced rate until full-retirement age and then switch to the other one at that time and receive an unreduced benefit.

One widow pointed out to me that widow(er)s who remarry before age sixty give up the right to collect benefits from the previous spouse's Social Security earnings unless the new marriage ends. So a widow or widower who begins dating again before age sixty may want to consider this information when planning a wedding date.

No Prorating of Benefits

Social Security benefits are not prorated during the month. If the worker does not survive the entire month, the Social Security benefit must be returned. In other words, there is no benefit payable for the month of death.

The benefits available to survivors through Social Security are complicated. Do not be afraid to ask questions or ask for a second opinion. If you seem to be getting conflicting insight, ask your financial consultant for an opinion. If your consultant is not familiar with the particular topic, he or she may have resources for finding a clearer answer.

Veterans Benefits

There are a number of benefits available to veterans' survivors depending upon the status of the veteran. One survivor pointed out the significant benefits his mother received as a result of his father's death being associated with his military service. Talk to the Department of Veteran Affairs to determine if there are benefits available for you or your loved ones.

Tip: Call 1-800-827-1000 to receive a copy of the Veterans Administration's free pamphlet *Summary of Department of Veteran Affairs Benefits.*

If you are a veteran, it is wise to have copies of your discharge papers along with your wills and other valuable documents. Some cemeteries offer discounted or complimentary plots for veterans.

Housing Decisions

Four bedrooms and two and a half bathrooms are plenty of room for a family of five or more. However, what if there are only one or two people living in the house? Is it the right size?

Consider downsizing while you are healthy.

The thought of downsizing can be a little unnerving, but it is worth considering while you are of sound mind. Often families defer consideration about downsizing until their mental or physical health is failing. The effort can become significantly more difficult at that time. If you are downsizing in a reactionary fashion, it is wise to evaluate downsizing twelve or more months after your spouse passes away.

Try to defer major decisions during your grief.

Ideally, you have discussed this issue and reviewed your best housing options before suffering a loss. This chapter is designed to make this evaluation process easier. If a loss has already occurred, it's a good idea to avoid major financial decisions, such as selling or buying a house, during the first few months after losing a loved one. Sometimes emotions can sway a quick decision, hindering one's ability to make the best long-term decision.

Housing decisions are difficult during normal circumstances, let alone when your health is failing or you have lost a loved one. Some want out as quickly as possible due to the memories that the house so frequently brings to mind; others cherish the house precisely because of the fond memories. The emotional component is certainly one factor to consider in your future housing needs.

There are a several options for the immediate housing decision and for the longer term. Listed below are some succinct descriptions of some common solutions. These are by no means the only possibilities. There may be better solutions for you than those listed in this summary; so keep an open mind as opportunities are presented.

Housing Issues to Review:

Stay Put

One consideration when deciding whether to stay in your current home or move is your own health, which may currently be changing. Typically a larger house requires more effort to navigate, clean, and maintain.

Webster defines *entropy* as the process of degradation or running down or trend to disorder. This physics principle is displayed as clearly in a house as in other objects. If you leave the yard alone for a couple weeks, you can generally see entropy in motion as the weeds and grass take over.

As entropy begins to take hold in a house, it can become an emotional burden for some. There seems to be a common sense of helplessness for those who are not gifted in maintaining their house.

Maintenance, mobility, and expense are important factors to consider as you review your current home.

Use caution when hiring contractors.

Consider the following:

- Maintaining your house requires a proactive approach, and the larger the house the more necessary activity is involved.
- Will you do the home maintenance work yourself?
- Will a family member do the home maintenance or will you hire someone to do it for you? If you hire someone, what will be the cost?
- As age takes its toll and it becomes progressively more difficult to complete tasks, who will you depend on to maintain your home?
- Do not be afraid to make a decision based on your home's state of disrepair. This feeling can lead to further dilapidation and frustration.

In past generations, family members lived in closer proximity and life was slower paced, allowing families to look after one another more effectively. Today, jobs require families to move great distances. The support is often limited to a smaller number of family members, and those who live in the area are pulled by a variety of demands on their time. So although family members may wish to help, they may be left with the frustration and guilt of not being able to do so.

Hiring Work Out

If you can no longer do the work necessary to maintain your house and if family members can offer only limited help, you may need to hire assistance. For many people this works out well. A good way to begin hiring the help you need is to talk with family and friends. Ask which individuals and agencies they recommend for specific jobs.

Chat with these prospective workers and get quotes for their work. By and large, contractors do not require prepayment, so if the workers are demanding such, it is best to consider someone else.

Consider the following:

- It is generally a bad idea to hire a person or company that happens to come to your front door. Many of the scams published in the paper are perpetrated by individuals who target the vulnerable, including widows, widowers, and those who are naïve about maintenance issues.
- Secure references from a contractor and call them to set an appointment to see a sample of the contractor's work. A common scam is to offer fictitious people as references with the hope you will only call about their work rather than attempt to see it in person. These so-called references (who are actually partners in crime) will say, "Oh, yes, Harry did a great job replacing my siding. I highly recommend him."
- If the contractor is not referred to you by a friend or family member, take your extra set of eyes to check out the contractor's past work.
- Get a second opinion or quote on work you are considering. The *lowest quote is not always the best*

solution. Securing multiple quotes will help you get a better read on market prices. If one is either much more expensive or much less expensive, beware there is probably a reason for the variance. You should call the contractor to see why the price seems out of line. If the price was low, it might be because the contractor had some free time and just needed some work. If the price was higher, it might be that the contractor may have seen a bigger problem than the others, something that might have been overlooked. Or the quotes might just be extreme.

The economics of contracting work out might be significant enough to lead you to consider moving. If your spouse was handy and took care of the maintenance around the homestead, you might be stunned to learn the additional cost necessary to hire professionals to take over that responsibility.

Move Decisions

If after an objective analysis of your situation you conclude it is time to move to a new house, the next step can be a little baffling. If you decide to move and are not certain about the future, consider adopting the mindset that moving may be a temporary solution. It will buy time for a more permanent solution and may relieve you of some pressure.

Your first move might be a temporary one.

The accumulation of a lifetime of belongings is a roadblock that prevents many from moving. But in order to effectively downsize to a different house, some household possessions must be given away. Those who are emotionally tied to the stuff they have accumulated often find the downsizing process to be more difficult.

Hopefully, Chapter 3 motivated you to start this process of downsizing so that when the moving decision is made there will be fewer possessions to have to pack and move. Without doing so, it is difficult to move a four-bedroom house into a two-bedroom version. If possible, work with loved ones to make this decision before experiencing a loss and start the process of inventorying and disposing of unneeded possessions. *This may be the most difficult aspect of moving.*

A number of years ago a physician, Dr. George pointed out to me how improved mobility within a house can add time to one's life. It seemed a little far-fetched to me, but as I quizzed him he pointed out how falls within the house often initiate a downward spiral in many people's health. Strive to maximize the mobility within your house by making passageways wider and free of furniture and other obstacles.

Consider the following:

- Remove the steps from a multilevel house to eliminate the biggest culprit behind falls. Being sensitive to the belongings you allow to clutter your new abode can help as well.
- Reduce the bulk from your home to simplify your lifestyle and diminish the number of things you are burdened to clean and dust.
- Go to the Tools and Tips section at *www.homeartisanauthority.com* for a list of ideas on how to age-proof a home if you are preparing a place for aging parents or ones who have recently been widowed.

Some reasonable housing solutions might include a smaller house, a condominium, an apartment, a retirement neighborhood townhome, moving in with a relative, or even an assisted living facility. These solutions all have pros and cons. Any of them can be transformed from a house to a home. A brief summary of each of these is listed below.

Patio Homes Simplify Things

If you consider moving into another house, a small, single-story ranch house might be a good choice.

Consider the following:

- Having your entire house on one floor makes it easier for one person to clean. If you're an older widow/widower, then a single floor patio home is easier on aging joints.

- A smaller house usually requires less time and effort to maintain. Often the smaller houses will have a smaller yard. Usually, patio homes have neighborhood associations to take care of the yard work.
- Living in a house maintains a level of privacy not afforded in an apartment or condominium. Additionally, owning a house might allow more room for your stuff.

Hey, Kids! I'm Moving In

There is a myth evolving in modern culture that it is a humiliating or severe imposition to move in with family members. I've heard it many times during my days. "I don't want to inconvenience my children. I don't want to move in with them. That would be asking too much of them." The ideas are similar, and they are based more on an outdated generational idea than on reality.

There have been few if any cultures in the history of the world in which the older generation did not become dependent upon the younger one later in life. The affluence of America has deluded many of us to believe, falsely, that it is an embarrassment to rely on family members during different seasons of life. If families cannot depend on one another to help with their needs, what really differentiates a family from any other group of people?

There are a number of ways family members can help with the housing needs of aging relatives. These ideas are intended to help you brainstorm and consider viable options.

Thirty years ago I traveled the local streets on my ten-speed bike depositing newspapers in the general vicinity of my customers' front doorsteps. One day I noticed that one family among my customers had begun a construction project on their garage. A few months later I received notice that I was to begin delivering a newspaper not only to my customer, but also to their former garage. It was then that I discovered a "mother-in-law's apartment." Today, the same concept is an ideal solution for a younger widow or widower trying to cope with a loss and raise children too.

Families are designed to help one another.

Mother-in-law apartments are an idea from the past.

- A unique variant is that the mother-in-law's house might be paid for whereas her children's home is not paid for. Maybe the mother-in-law would be willing to live in a smaller portion of her house and allow the next generation to take over the rest. This might be a win-win situation for all. It's a different but not totally new idea.
- It is reasonable to believe children might have more house than necessary and could convert a section to meet the needs of an aging or recently widowed parent or a single-parent widow or widower who is finding it difficult to navigate life alone. This would include expenditure of time and money, but it can provide incredible blessings to all involved.
- Sometimes adult siblings move in together. In this scenario the siblings look after one another in case of an accident or health problems and share the housework so that there is less work per person. This allows all parties to share expenses and provides incredible social benefits too. It might require one person to relocate, but it often works with remarkable success.
- Another possibility is for adult children to buy a condominium next to their parents. It can be an efficient housing solution that simultaneously allows for autonomy and support.

Condominium arrangements allow you to delegate much of the upkeep involved in home ownership.

The Joys of a Condominium

A condominium is usually a house in which the interior is owned by the individual while all of the exterior surfaces, including the yard, are owned by a common group of people. Condominiums are available in all price ranges and sizes, so you might be able to find one to meet your needs.

- Monthly condo fees often cover the outside expenses of the entire neighborhood. These fees should be reviewed carefully before you commit to a location as they may increase over time due to inflation. All fees and costs should be considered in regard to a monthly budget.
- Beware: some condominiums save money for large expenses like new roofs, whereas others just charge substantial assessments when big expenses arise. It is important to determine which accounting practices the condo you are considering implements. The condos that accrue each year for larger expenses tend to pass the expense to the current owner and not unsuspecting future owners.
- Some of the positive aspects about owning a condominium include home ownership without the burden of overseeing property maintenance outside of your individual unit. Additionally, neighbors in condominiums tend to be less transient than those in apartments.
- Because you own the condo, you have the liberty to make changes inside the unit within the confines of the association guidelines, which makes it a little easier to convert it from a house to a home.

Apartment living can be a temporary solution for your housing decisions.

How About an Apartment?

Renting an apartment seems to have a bad rap. However, there may be good reasons to consider renting rather than owning property.

Consider the following:

- Renting an apartment can be a temporary solution to allow you time to consider your long-term desires. Apartments may offer short-term leases as brief as six months, but they normally extend twelve months. The choice to rent an apartment allows the equity from your house to earn interest to offset some of your rent.

Storage units allow you to subdivide your belongings temporarily.

- A unique benefit of renting an apartment is that it allows a tenant to delegate all maintenance, both inside and outside, to the owner of the property. There is no need to shovel, mow, and repair the air conditioner, the stove or the hot water heater; all of those responsibilities are included in your monthly rent.
- Apartments usually offer extended savings because utilities are often included in the rent and there are no property taxes.
- If you decide to rent an apartment as a transitional alternative to purchasing other real estate, you can always rent a self-storage unit to store possessions you wish to keep that don't fit in the apartment. This simplifies your downsizing efforts and you still keep your belongings intact.
- The selection of an apartment should meet your social expectations. As a younger survivor, it might be best to rent an apartment with others in your age group to make it easier to transition through the changes ahead. Likewise, if you are a retirement-aged survivor then a complex targeted to retirees may have a number of scheduled activities better suited to your lifestyle.

Talk to friends about their moving experiences to learn some tips.

Assisted Living

The idea of assisted living might seem scary, but it may be the perfect choice for individuals who want to live independently if they currently need a little help with some activities of daily living (ADL) or if they are just planning ahead for that time. Examples of ADL include bathing, eating, housekeeping, managing medication, and the like.

Consider the following:

- Assisted living services vary across the board among facilities. The facilities range from small apartments to townhome-type mini homes. The menu of services available varies significantly and can include amenities such as meal preparation, prescription help, and medical assistance. The services are similar to a menu at a restaurant; you choose the ones you need and pay accordingly.

- This housing option offers some social interaction not necessarily available in other choices. Frequently the community has activities and shuttle bus services to malls, groceries stores, retail centers, and other points of interest.
- Assisted living may be a choice that defers the need to consider a nursing home facility. This choice may be safer for many individuals, allowing them to live healthier, more active lives. As your health changes, incremental services can be added.
- This option is similar to living in an apartment. Generally, you do not own the property but instead rent it from a landlord who is responsible for the maintenance inside and out. Assisted living facilities vary broadly across the country. It is difficult to compare one facility to another without standard criteria. This Web link offers a comprehensive checklist to help in your efforts: www.fpeca.cas.usf.edu/chltc/PDF_Files/ALFEVAL.pdf.

Sorting Through the Choices

Whether you choose to stay in your home, move to a smaller house, live with a family member, rent an apartment, select a condominium, or even consider an assisted living facility, the decision is very personal and dependent on your specific desires. You may find it easier to arrive at the best decision by involving a family member or close friend in the discussions about the pros and cons of each option. If at all possible, talk to people who have gone through the process before you. They can tell you what they learned.

Ultimately, housing is simply a place for shelter. As long as you have friends, family, and loved ones, the location or color of your kitchen, living room, and bedroom are not nearly as important. Remember downsizing is best done in a proactive mode while there are fewer emotional components involved in the decision.

Working Again

Work is equated with punishment in some circles, but work offers some incredible and often underestimated benefits to individuals. There is a sense of accomplishment and value derived from investing one's time and talent in a productive effort. There are also incredible friendships developed in the work environment.

Work is honorable.

In the absence of work, there is often a sense of uselessness that can be overwhelming if other activities do not fill the void. Jim D. Pinkston, CFP®, a financial consultant, tells his clients, "Work is honorable." Work does not have to include compensation. There are an infinite number of places that can use your skills and ways you can invest time, including voluntary roles. However, sometimes economics or circumstances may indicate the *need* to return to work even if you were previously retired.

Consider the following:

- The need to work is not an immediate concern after losing a loved one, but it may become evident in the weeks that follow. Before you consider returning to work, review your budget and net worth statement to determine your income needs and work options.

  For example, if there is a cash flow shortage of $800 monthly after taxes, it is likely you will need to earn $1,000 to $1,200 monthly before taxes. Knowing that number before you begin talking with potential employers is crucial.

  At $7.50 an hour, one would need to work nearly full time to generate the required income. Some $7.50 hourly jobs allow the ability to leave the work behind at the end of the day, but the lower stress jobs may require more hours to earn the amount you need. However, a job paying $15 hourly would require you to work only twenty hours weekly to take care of your cash flow. Unfortunately there are fewer part-time jobs that are low-stress *and* pay $15 hourly.

- You might need to go back to work simply to integrate more social contact back into your life rather than because of a cash flow concern. In this situation it makes sense to pursue a job in an area that is a hobby for you. This allows you to spend your time doing something you like and provides you the opportunity to meet others with similar interests.

- Another condition that might require you to return to work is the need to receive health insurance benefits. If this is the case, you will need to pursue employers who offer health insurance at a cost that is reasonable for you.
- There are also therapeutic reasons to work. One widow told me, "Work was the best medicine for me. I needed to be with people during the healing process."

Whatever the motive for returning to work, try to adjust your mindset in advance from "I have to go to work" to "I get to return to work." There are no guarantees any of us will ever be assured of never having to work again and yet there is a temptation to feel bad if one must return to work after retirement.

Today, there are many job opportunities available. Your attitude will likely affect your performance and pay, not to speak of your enjoyment. Talk to friends who are still working; maybe they have found an employer who has a friendly work environment and might need more help. This will make it easier to integrate back into the marketplace.

Consider working in a role associated with one of your hobbies.

Updating Your Documents and Accounts

Flossing is an interruption. It seems as though the only person who cares if you floss is your dental hygienist. Similarly, preparing estate documents, beneficiary designations, accounts, and account registrations can be tedious and outwardly unrewarding activities. It seems only your financial advisor cares if you accomplish this task.

However, updating these records makes life easier for your loved ones to act on your behalf should you become disabled or pass away. Outdated, missing, or inaccurate documents could result in your lifelong efforts of financial management causing great strain on those closest to you or yielding great rewards to people you never intended. *Updating these records is a loving and caring effort made for the people who are important to you!*

Updated documents increase the likelihood of your financial wishes being fulfilled.

Prepare Now for Tomorrow

Here's a checklist of suggested documents and tasks to prepare, review, and update in advance. Taking this step will save you and your loved ones legal fees, reduce stress, and possibly diminish the impact of taxes too.

- Wills
- Trusts
- Health-care directives
- Power of attorney documents
- Designate beneficiaries (primary and secondary)
- Insurance records, retirement plans, and any other accounts with beneficiaries

Wills, Trusts, and Such

Within weeks of your passing, your loved ones will need to begin processing your estate. This can be challenging and may take many forms depending on your use of joint accounts, beneficiary-designated accounts, wills, and trusts. Normally, emotions are supercharged, and much of the legal jargon often sounds like a foreign language.

This procedure is much easier if you update critical documents in advance. STOP: Go find your wills or trusts and take time to read them right now! Scribble notes in the margins where you see changes that are necessary. Whether you have a will, living trust, or health-care directives and powers of attorney, you likely have changes that have occurred since the documents were originally drafted. Review these same legal documents with your loved ones before you experience a loss to ensure you and everyone you love has a basic understanding of the meaning and intent of each document.

Tip: It's a good idea to have someone you trust read your will, trust, and other critical documents and then have them share their interpretation of them to test the clarity of the documents.

Encourage your loved ones, upon experiencing a loss, to bring a confidante along to the attorney meetings to listen to the conversations and help ask pertinent questions. *Let your heirs know that they are under no obligation to use the services of the attorney who originally drafted your documents to administer your estate.*

The Attorney Works for You and Your Heirs

Let your attorney know you want clear communication that you can understand, and encourage your loved ones to except nothing less. You are ultimately the attorney's employer, and if that attorney cannot work in a fashion that meets your expectations, there are plenty of others who would be happy to help. Do not accept service that makes you feel intimidated about asking questions and getting answers to issues you don't understand.

Remember that closing an estate can take six to twelve months for simple situations and even longer for more complex estates. Advance preparation usually diminishes problems that delay this process. Once started, remember that closing an estate is reliant upon collecting information from a variety of sources; it doesn't hurt to check in briefly with your attorney on a regular basis to make sure the attorney has everything necessary to proceed. *The squeaky wheel gets the oil.*

Update Your Documents Now

This is an excellent time for your attorney to update your final documents. If you did the exercise above, you have the initial ideas for necessary changes already noted on your existing documents.

While updating your will or trust, make sure your beneficiary designations are accurate. If you included timing of any distributions of your wealth, review whether it is still necessary and reasonable.

The term "per stirpes" means to pass a particular beneficiary's inheritance on to his or her offspring if the beneficiary predeceases you. Its use can be helpful to make sure grandchildren or nieces and nephews receive assets intended for their parents, should their parents die before being able to provide for those offspring themselves.

Power of Attorney Documents

Power of attorney (POA) documents are proactive initiatives that allow you the decision to name the person or persons you trust the most to act wisely on your behalf. They are a critical component of the financial planning process.

A power of attorney document can assign as little or as much power to the one you choose to help you. But without one in place when the time comes that your loved ones need to act on your behalf, they will have to work in a more emotionally charged environment and at a greater cost.

One attorney recently reported that it would take at least forty-five days to get a guardianship assigned by the court and could easily cost up to $5,000. Conversely a power of attorney costs a small fraction of that amount and is available immediately when there is a need.

Your attorney should communicate in language you understand and in a way with which you feel comfortable.

It is best to get the documents in place while you are healthy so you will not have the emotions of your own health affecting the process. Power of attorney documents are fairly standard and an attorney should be able to draft one for your review in a few days.

The person I would trust with power of attorney is an individual who is wise, compassionate, and honest. That person would qualify to be the overseer of my affairs in my absence. You need to not only define the type of person for yourself but also identify the specific person who fits that bill and ideally a backup or two.

It's best to discuss the roles with the individuals in advance of naming them. You should also empower them in advance verbally. They may need to make decisions on your behalf that you cannot comprehend due to emotions, illness, or other difficult situations. Tell them it is OK. Remember you are looking for someone wise, compassionate, and honest.

You may need to name new primary and secondary people to fulfill the roles in your power of attorney and health-care documents as circumstances change. It is trickier when you fill those responsibilities with non-spouse individuals.

Allowing someone control over your personal material and your health is a very trusting consideration. Make sure you are aware of the rights that those individuals will receive as a result of being granted this power, and make certain that you are comfortable allowing those individuals to have this kind of control.

Timely Documents Are Important

The decisions you make when you update your documents do not have to be final. It is better to get as close as possible to defining your wishes with signed documents than to have old documents that no longer mirror your wishes. You can continue to amend your documents as you gain more clarity. Your financial consultant should be willing to join you for meetings with your attorney to help review your documents.

Power of attorney rights are significant; be sure you understand what you are assigning.

Beneficiary designations override instructions in wills and trusts.

Updating Beneficiary Forms on Insurance and Retirement Plans

Beneficiaries designated on insurance policies and retirement plans override the designations of beneficiaries within your will or trust. Often the beneficiary on these accounts is a spouse or other loved one.

Probate certifies the legality of a will, making it easier to attend to the assets and affairs of deceased individuals. Probate procedures vary from state to state. Costs associated with the process include attorneys' fees, both for attorneys representing an estate and for the court overseeing the effort. The process can lead to delays in separating assets if all your documents are not in order. This can result in more worry and often undue additional expenses for those left behind.

Review the designations annually. If your spouse is the only one listed as a beneficiary and something happens to both of you, the entire account could end up passing through probate unnecessarily and costing your heirs more in taxes and legal fees.

Use primary and secondary beneficiary designations.

A great checklist to use with this is your net worth statement. Generally, all of the assets within the category "retirement assets" include beneficiary designations. The life insurance policies listed at the bottom of the net worth statement should also list beneficiaries.

The financial institution representing each account can provide a written summary of the existing beneficiaries along with a change of beneficiary form. Your financial consultant can track these down on your behalf. To save some time and energy, enlist your consultant to help you tend to these matters before a loss.

It is important to name both primary and secondary (or contingent) beneficiaries. This is critical in case something happens to your primary beneficiary *and* you before you are able to update the necessary change of beneficiary forms. Your financial consultant can explain the alternatives available in naming beneficiaries and can work along with your attorney to align beneficiary designations with your other estate plans and wishes.

Use caution when handling retirement accounts.

If you are the beneficiary of an IRA or retirement plan and the spouse of the deceased, you generally have the option to roll the assets into an IRA in your name. However, if you are younger than fifty-nine and a half, there may be some benefits to keeping them in a beneficiary IRA to provide more flexibility. *Discuss this topic with your financial consultant before you make any decisions.*

New rules make the formerly unique opportunity available within IRAs available in 401(k) plans. Non-spouse beneficiaries now have the option to consider distributions from IRAs and 401(k) plans in three distinct ways. *Your 401(k) should allow the three options below once the balance is rolled into an IRA.* But keep in mind that some employers do not add all of the new benefits available by law to their unique 401(k) plans, so check with them to assure you understand what flexibility is offered through their plans. Any distributions made to a beneficiary are not subject to a 10 percent penalty prior to age fifty-nine and a half, but they will be subject to ordinary income taxes.

The Non-Spouse Beneficiary Can:

1. Take the entire balance from the inherited IRA in a lump-sum distribution. This option is a good one if you think the beneficiary will be in need of money immediately or if the account is relatively small. This choice will generally result in the highest immediate income tax.
2. Take the entire balance out by the end of the fifth year following the year of the owner's death. If this choice is elected, no distribution is required before the end of the fifth year. This choice often provides more flexibility in tax planning than the lump-sum option provides.
3. Take distributions based on his or her life expectancy in the year following the death of the owner and each year thereafter. This generally allows the beneficiary to defer taxes for the longest period of time with the potential of receiving more income. It requires recalculating the required minimum distribution annually and allows the flexibility to take more than the amount if necessary.

Issues pertinent to receiving an IRA or 401(k) as a beneficiary may inflict significant income taxes upon you. Before you act, be sure to discuss the choices with your tax advisor.

As you discuss beneficiary designations with your financial consultant, you might discuss the benefits of using different registration titles on your accounts. Refer to the discussion of account registrations in the following section if you have preliminary questions.

Account Registrations

There are several ways investments, savings accounts, and other assets can be registered. The method you choose can affect the ownership, taxation, and ease of transfer to the intended beneficiary.

Typically the registration of an account appears on the monthly statement. Sometimes it's necessary to have the financial institution review its records to verify the actual registration.

As you review the registrations of your accounts, update them to assure they are in line with your goals. Delaying this effort now could make it more complicated later. Listed below are some of the more commonly used registrations, along with a brief description and example of each.

Proper registration of accounts is important.

Individual Ownership

Individual ownership (e.g., George W. Green) is a frequent registration an individual might use to register his or her accounts. Married couples might use this registration to balance out marital assets for estate planning purposes or to limit liability. The owner is responsible for the asset and has full control over it. Upon the owner's death, the asset is part of his or her estate and is subject to probate.

Joint Tenancy with Rights of Survivorship (JTWROS)

This registration (e.g., Betsy R. and George W. Green) reflects an asset owned by two or more individuals with equal ownership. Whoever is a joint owner has complete control over the entire account independent of the other(s). Consequently one of the disadvantages of JTWROS is a diluted control of the asset.

For example, if a mother were to add her daughter as a JTWROS owner, her daughter could legally withdraw the money from the account. The daughter subsequently might have to find a new location for Thanksgiving dinner, but her actions would be legal. Additionally, if the daughter were sued or went through a divorce, the JTWROS assets might be subject to the legal proceeding.

When one joint owner dies, his or her share of the asset passes directly to the other joint owner(s) proportionately without passing through probate. This can often result in one child receiving the entire remaining balance to the exclusion of that child's siblings, which often may not be the intent of the original account owner.

Tenancy in Common

Tenancy in common (e.g., Betsy R. (40 percent) and George W. Green (60 percent) as Cotenants) exists among two or more co-owners and is a blend between JTWROS and individual ownership. It allows individuals to merge assets and yet maintain their proportionate ownership. There does not need to be equal ownership, as the example above displays.

At death, the ownership percentages remain the same. The decedent's ownership passes to his or her other beneficiaries subject to probate.

JTWROS allows direct distribution to the surviving owners.

Transfer on Death (TOD)

Transfer on death (e.g., George W. Green TOD George W. Green, Jr.) wording can be added to an individual ownership or JTWROS registration. The addition of this wording to an account has the effect of a beneficiary designation form you might find on a retirement account or insurance policy. It allows the assets to pass directly to the intended beneficiary without the necessity of probate.

The named beneficiary under a TOD arrangement has no ownership rights to the account during the owner's lifetime. It allows the original owner to maintain full control and yet distribute the assets directly to his or her named beneficiary on death. Sometimes Pay on Death (POD) is used in a similar fashion (e.g., George W. Green POD George W. Green, Jr.).

TOD works similar to beneficiary designated assets.

Custodian

Ownership of assets is generally contingent upon a contractual agreement. Because minors are not legally able to sign contracts, it's necessary to have a person of majority age make legal agreements on behalf of minors.

A common registration to accomplish this is a custodial agreement (e.g., George W. Green, as Custodian for George W. Green, Jr. under the Indiana Uniform Transfer to Minors Act [UTMA]). In a custodial agreement there is only one person of majority age allowed on each account along with the minor. The age of majority is unique to each state, but it is usually eighteen or twenty-one. Each state offers one or both of the following types of custodial accounts: UTMA or Uniform Gift to Minors Act (UGMA).

Assets in this registration are legally owned by the minor, and the adult has the responsibility to invest them in a prudent fashion. Income is reportable on the minor's tax return.

Trust

An account registered in the name of a trust will allow it to operate according to the trust document during and after the lifetime of the individual who funded it. There are a variety of trusts available, so the registrations will vary depending on the type of trust.

The trust document designates who controls the account (the trustee) and outlines the parameters of distribution of assets and income throughout the duration of the trust, along with other pertinent information. One of the more common trusts is a revocable living trust. It is an effective method of transferring assets to the appropriate parties after the original owner's death (e.g., The George W. Green Revocable Living Trust, dated 1/1/07, Trustees George W. Green and Betsy R. Green).

The method you choose to register an asset can have significant tax implications. Therefore, it is important to work alongside a professional with a good working knowledge of the pros and cons of each particular choice.

Consider this example: Thelma and Ralph bought one hundred shares of a small company named Microsoft in 1985 in JTWROS. Somehow they forgot about this little investment and as the years rolled on they realized they had accumulated 28,800 shares. Their cost basis is roughly $2,500.

Sadly, Ralph has been given a diagnosis of terminal cancer and has begun to fight for his life. Although it might seem a little distasteful, it might make sense to register many of the shares in his name. His illness may have increased the likelihood he will predecease Thelma. Should that come to pass, all of the shares in his name will have a step-up in cost basis upon his death to the date of death value, should he live twelve months after the transfer. This effort could possibly save Thelma thousands in capital gains taxes.

This is an example of one option to consider. You need to review your situation with your loved ones, financial advisor, accountant, and attorney before you act to determine the best option(s) for you. It is important to proactively register all of your accounts.

Get Your Bearings

Don't make hasty financial decisions. After a loss there is a tendency to get caught up in distracting busy work, which may lead you to make quick decisions you'll regret later. First survey your situation.

The nautical term "bearings" involves the idea of determining your location and destination in order to maneuver successfully in open waters even when there are no shorelines to help guide you. Guiding a boat through open water while the shoreline is in sight is relatively easy, but if the shoreline disappears, all bets are off.

The loss of a loved one may have a similar effect. It can disrupt one's perspective and cause a sense of disorientation, much like being lost on open water without landmarks to guide you. When you've lost your bearings, it's a good idea to stop and get a sense of direction before moving forward to avoid jeopardizing the welfare of your financial situation.

This chapter is designed to point out some common frustrations thrust upon people when they begin looking at new financial issues as a survivor and to allow you insight to better prepare the way. Your survivors will need to first review their current condition and then proceed from a clearer state of mind. But with regard to their financial well-being, it is best for them to move deliberately and survey their situation with trusted advisors before making any significant decisions.

Urgent Decisions

Many of the topics discussed so far will help minimize the urgent decisions your survivors may face. Unfortunately, though, some of the most difficult decisions in life are the urgent ones. You know the type; there is no time to sleep on it, no time to ask others for their insight, no time to delay the decision in any way whatsoever. These decisions often leave plenty of room for mistakes, frustrations, anxiety and regret.

As for your survivors, there should be very few, if any, of these types of decisions. The most urgent decisions they may have to attend to are the final funeral arrangements. Beyond those decisions, persuade them to take their time.

There are people who would lead you or your heirs to believe a decision is necessary immediately, but in reality, time is on your and your heirs' side. In fact, if someone is pressing for a quick decision, it is a good indicator that the person is not considering your survivors' best interests.

Some common sources of unnecessary pressure might come from other family members, former employers, financial advisors, and salespersons. If you run a family business, the pressure may come from company employees. If someone continues to press for a decision, question the person to determine the source of his or her urgency. Ask, for example, "If I don't decide now, what is the worst that will happen?" or "What do you have to gain from me making a decision?" or "Why is it so important for me to make the decision right now?"

Recently a widow friend called the office, stressed immeasurably, with a concern about her health-care benefits from her husband's former employer. A friend of the family who worked with her husband called earlier in the morning and told her she needed to get to the employer that day or she would lose her health insurance.

My assistant postponed my other scheduled meetings to free up my time so that I could be this woman's extra set of ears during a meeting with the employer. Within minutes we determined the widow had health insurance and was not required to make a decision for thirty days.

In this example, the person who initiated the urgency was an educated executive who seemed to have the widow's best interests in mind. However, the result was that the widow experienced unnecessary emotional stress.

Many well-intentioned people may offer opinions or thoughts, but it becomes increasingly important to rely on experts and professionals to help you and your loved ones to weave your way through the decision process and keep things in perspective. This is especially true for survivors who are unable to proactively complete the steps in this guide and are therefore feeling pressured to do so after a loss.

If you or your heirs can afford to defer economic-related decisions, it is probably best to allow several months to pass before making any major decisions. There is no need to immediately call a real estate agent or to plan to move, unless time has been taken to think through the process and plan for the variables involved far in advance. One widow relayed it this way: "The first year I was in shock. The second year reality kicked in and it was time to move on."

Involving a trusted extra set of ears when discussions about decisions are initiated will offer extra security. The other person will likely be less emotional about the information presented.

> **Allow as much time as possible before making critical decisions to help minimize the influence of emotions.**

It's All Greek to Me

The financial services industry is notorious for overwhelming consumers with mail. Ideally, you will spend time with loved ones to sift through these types of documents before experiencing a loss. This will familiarize you and those you love with the kind of materials they will need to sort through, organize, interpret, and act on should a death occur. This summary is designed to help streamline the process for those who are new to processing statements and other mailings of this type.

Some financial mail is junk mail!

Don't get overwhelmed by the mail. There's a temptation for newcomers to this process to believe they're the only ones on the planet who don't understand the information that fills the mailbox. It's doubtful anyone understands everything received from financial institutions, so please don't be intimidated.

Whether you are doing this in advance or after suffering a loss, a good starting place is to sort your financial mail into four piles initially—bills, statements, requests for action, and informative documents. Each of these piles can be efficiently processed and filed appropriately with a little practice.

Bills

Generally your loved ones will receive only a few bills from your financial institutions. If this is their first cycle for paying the bill, they should take time to call your financial professional to gain an understanding of what it represents and whether it is a necessary bill.

Verify whether a bill is authentic. If you are unsure, ask your financial consultant to review it.

Some examples of bills from your financial institutions might be the following: auto, homeowners, life or disability insurance premiums; annual fees; quarterly fees; and loan payments.

As they review the invoices, suggest they make notes of the due dates and any incremental fees that will be assessed if payment is late. It's important to get answers to these questions prior to the due date. If the specific financial institution is not as helpful as necessary, your financial consultant should be able to help them sort through the specifics.

Normally it is safe to shred the bill once confirmation of payment is credited to the appropriate account. There is no need to keep paid bills indefinitely.

Statements

Many financial institutions generate monthly statements, whereas others send quarterly or annual statements. The frequency varies among organizations.

It might be helpful to create a file for each financial institution and store the most recent statement in front of the previous statement. This filing system enables a quick comparison of the balance and transactions from last month or the month before to the current month. Comparing statements from month to month is a good way to become familiar with them and gain an understanding of transaction flow. Use a highlighter to mark areas that are difficult to understand.

Make notes next to the highlighted areas for reference to review with your financial consultant.

Encourage your loved ones to look closely at the first statements they begin to review for any electronic transactions that are set up for automatic payment. You could even include a summary of automatic transactions to help them. This could be updated annually with your other important documents. If automatic transactions are no longer valid, they will need to make it a priority to discontinue them.

There is a tendency to want to keep all statements and records from all accounts. But with the electronic culture today, it's very easy for most financial institutions to regenerate past statements. Initially it is probably best to keep statements for a couple of years to create a little history and reference point for each account. Once your heirs have become familiar with the statements, your financial consultant can explain how to discard the statements and identify those that are necessary to keep.

Emphasize the importance of shredding any financial documents that are no longer needed. *Your financial consultant should be able to shred the documents.*

Requests for Action

The advent of high-speed printers and databases has allowed financial institutions to generate mailings faster and more furiously than at any other time in history. Additionally, the increased regulatory requirements by state and federal agencies require financial organizations to frequently update their records.

A request for action does not necessarily mean action is required. Some entities send out proxies, a technical term for a ballot that allows investors to vote for certain corporate issues, or surveys to determine client views, which are not required but are merely helpful to the financial institution. During a transition period, it might be time saving to simply shred optional requests.

Most statements can be saved electronically to streamline your records.

You don't have to respond to all requests for information or votes!

Tip: As your loved ones process documents received from financial institutions, it's critical to determine whether they're legitimate. There are people who prey on grieving individuals and responding to illegitimate documents can give scam artists access to your information. A good place to start is to make sure each *request for action* is from a financial institution that has also sent a statement. If a past statement identifying the organization that sent you the request can't be found, your heirs should give your financial consultant a quick call to explain the request and ask for advice.

Mandatory requests usually have strict deadlines printed in bold on the form and often include a return envelope. Again, if your heirs are in doubt whether returning the form is necessary, your financial consultant should be able to assist. It's a good idea to pay attention to requests for action, determine whether or not they are pertinent, and either process or shred them accordingly.

Tip: *Beware:* There is a high-tech method to request for action known as *phishing*. It is an illegitimate request for information via electronic communication used by criminals whose main objective is to steal identity. *Do not offer any personal information to organizations that request it via email. Call their service center using the phone number on your most recent statement to verify the request's legitimacy.*

Criminals are willing to steal yours and your loved ones' identities through phishing; they are even bold enough to call directly on the phone and pose as a legitimate bank or other financial institution. Do not give information over the phone to people no matter how legitimate they sound. Ask them for their name and phone number. They will likely hang up when asked for this information.

Informative Documents

Informative documents are often helpful and educational, but they are not urgent or necessary. They generally are printed on glossy paper and do not include a name or personal information within them. Consequently they are the easiest to recognize as unnecessary.

If your heirs just can't handle discarding these documents, they should try the next best exercise—streamlining the documents kept. For example, if an eight-page document is received, flip through it and tear out the pages that are most appropriate to keep and discard the others.

A few years ago, my grandmother was bedridden. My uncle spent much of his free time helping her and let his mail get behind a little longer than normal. In less than ninety days, he had more than three garbage bags of informative documents. Don't be afraid to throw such documents away.

When in doubt, give your financial consultant a quick call. The office personnel often can help sift through the mail more quickly and efficiently. Some financial consultants even allow their clients to bring their mail in and help sort through it. Your financial advisor is there to help as much as possible and will understand your need for extra assistance during this time.

Inventory Your Situation

If you are reading this in a proactive manner, it is important to remember that no one really knows who will die first. Therefore, if you are married, or have been designated with power of attorney for your parents, it is a good idea to have periodic review sessions.

A helpful gift you can leave for your loved ones is an updated net worth statement along with an annualized spending plan (budget). A net worth statement is simply a list of everything you own and everything you owe. Once you subtract your debts from your assets, it gives the value of your true ownership or your "net worth."

The spending plan (budget) allows your survivors the opportunity to gauge the cash flow needs compared with the resources available to provide for them. A more detailed discussion of spending plans is included later in this chapter. Without a recent spending plan, it will

Update your net worth statement and spending plan at least annually and occasionally review them with your spouse.

likely take a few months for them to piece together a reasonable estimate of the monthly expenses and consequently delay the time they can get settled into a new lifestyle—unless you use software like Quicken or Money to manage your checkbook. If you do use budgeting software, be sure to *make your passwords known to your survivors.* Otherwise, the data may not be available to them. The Action Box provided (below) is a useful tool for achieving this task.

Occasionally, I ask my clients random questions to get to know them better. Recently I asked, "Suppose you are on a plane to Tahiti. You are ninety years old and the pilot says you only have one minute, one phone call, and one sentence to tell your loved ones the most important information about life. What would you tell them?"

One client answered in a rapid-fire manner, "My passwords and usernames are…." Don't underestimate the value of having that information available for your family.

The Action Box (below) can be a good starting point for noting your passwords. Be sure to keep it in a secure place once it is completed and update it as frequently as possible.

Passwords and User Names

Computer Sign-On _____

Internet _____

Financial Sites
(site, username,
password) _____

_____

_____

_____

Miscellaneous
Passwords _____

_____

_____

_____

Additionally, ask your financial advisor to scan your important documents, year-end statements, wills, trusts, military releases, and so forth, store them in electronic files, and provide you a copy. You can then provide that disk or copies to the appropriate people.

Updating Your Net Worth

Ideally your net worth statement will have at least three columns and a list of the specific assets. The three columns allow you to list the assets owned by the wife, the husband, and those that are in joint name. Such a document is helpful for a number of reasons. It will help your surviving spouse understand what assets are available to meet continuing financial needs. It will help the financial consultant review the family's situation and provide insight to the survivor(s). And it will also be helpful to any legal counsel that is completing necessary documents and tax forms.

Net Worth Statement

Date:				
	Wife	Husband	Joint	Total
ASSETS:				
Current Assets:				
Checking				
Savings				
Money Market				
Life Insurance (Cash Value)				
Other				
Total Current Assets:				
Intermediate Assets:				
CDs				
Stocks				
Stock Options				
Mutual Funds				
Other				
Total Intermediate Assets:				
Retirement Assets:				
401(k)				
IRAs				
Annuities				
Other				
Total Retirement Assets:				

	Wife	Husband	Joint	Total
Fixed Assets:				
Residence				
Other Real Estate				
Businesses				
Automobiles				
Furnishings				
Collectibles				
Total Fixed Assets:				
TOTAL ASSETS:				
LIABILITIES:				
Home Mortgages				
Auto Loans				
Credit Cards				
Other				
TOTAL LIABILITIES:				
NET WORTH:				
Life Insurance				
Income				

Use the Net Worth Statement above to inventory your current situation. It's helpful to update this document annually. A good time to update is after receiving all of your year-end statements every winter. A spending plan worksheet is included next to help summarize your expenses.

Complete the Net Worth Statement on the previous pages and the Spending Plan worksheet on the following page.

It's a good idea to keep your current and past net worth statements in the file where you keep your investment statements.

If you examine the Net Worth Statement, you will notice there are two distinct sections: assets and liabilities. Generally speaking, keeping the liability section as close to zero as possible helps reduce financial stress. But before paying off any debts, be sure to sit down with your financial advisor to find the best assets to use.

Some credit card companies include a life insurance policy within their accounts, and the balances might be automatically paid off upon the death of the cardholder. *Be sure to verify whether this is the situation with each financial institution and make a footnote on your net worth statement to better inform your loved ones.*

Spending Plans

"Who needs a budget?" "We've never used a budget." "A budget is too restrictive." "With our income, we don't need a budget." "A budget is too difficult to stick to." "We would never have gotten where we are today without a budget." "I know where every penny goes." "Our budget has kept us out of trouble." "If it's not in the budget, we don't buy it."

Do any of these statements sound like something you have said? Working with many families over the years, I've heard many different responses in regard to budgets. One thing is for certain: budgets seem to polarize peoples' opinions.

Webster defines a budget as a plan for the coordination of resources and expenditures. But budgets are so feared an entity that we call them *spending plans* to keep some people from going into to convulsions over the word *budget*. What is the truth about budgets? Are they a good thing or a bad thing? The answer is they are neutral. For some families a budget is necessary and helpful, and for others it is unnecessary.

Spending Plan

HOUSING		SAVINGS	
Mortgage (P&I)/Rent			
Utilities		**DISCRETIONARY EXPENSES**	
Yard Care		Dining Out	
Home Improvements		Club Dues	
TOTAL HOUSING		Paper/Magazines	
		Cable/Internet/Cell	
FOOD (Groceries)		Travel/Vacations	
CLOTHING/DRY CLEANING		Hobbies	
CAR		Religious	
		Charitable	
OTHER COMMITTED EXPENSES		Gifts (Birthday, Christmas)	
Education Costs		**TOTAL DISCRETIONARY**	
Hair Cuts			
Medical Expenses		**TAX PAYMENTS**	
Veterinary		Federal	
Miscellaneous		State	
TOTAL OTHER EXPENSES		Local	
		FICA	
LIABILITIES		Real Estate	
Charge Accounts		Licenses	
Bank Loan(s)		**TOTAL TAXES**	
Equity Loan(s)			
Auto Loan(s)		**TOTAL EXPENSES**	
Personal Loan(s)			
TOTAL LIABILITIES		**TOTAL INCOME**	
INSURANCE		**DISCRETIONARY INCOME**	
		(Total Income-Total Expenses)	

It's a good idea for all families to inventory spending from time to time, more or less for a gut check. It's very easy to allow spending to escalate without realizing it. The small additions of expenses may not seem like much by themselves, but cumulatively they can add a burden to your life.

There is an old saying: "Yesterday's luxuries become today's necessities." Less than ten years ago, very few families had cell phones and Internet service. Today these services are common. If a cell phone runs $30 and Internet service is $20 monthly, people utilizing those services easily add $600 annually to their budget without giving much thought to how that impacts their financial situation.

A budget can be an inventory of your annualized spending.

Whether you choose to budget daily, weekly, monthly, or annually, it is a good idea to review your expenditures to verify you are living within your means. If you are exceeding your income, there are corrective measures you can implement to reduce your future pain. If budgeting becomes a serious problem, make sure you bring it to your financial consultant's attention. There are a number of excellent organizations that are skilled at helping families with this area of their finances.

Source: Dave Ramsey's Financial Peace University (*www.daveramsey.com*) has received good reviews in the industry.

Help Is on the Way

Grief can have the effect of isolating people and making them feel alone. Furthermore, transitioning through the grief while addressing new responsibilities can be overwhelming. Even social interaction can be difficult for many.

One of the challenges during a time of loss may be asking for help and knowing whom to trust. This chapter encourages you to seek out help before a loss and offers some ideas about how to screen the professionals you are considering working with in advance.

Finding the Right Financial Consultant

Before you commit to any offers to help from professional advisors, take time to evaluate their capabilities and how they interact with you. Like a good doctor, a good financial consultant can be very useful to the fiscal health of a family. *A high-caliber financial consultant can streamline the estate planning process—reducing both the time spent on financial matters and the stress money-related decisions often have on survivors.*

It is a good idea to choose and work through issues and questions with a trusted financial consultant in advance of the death of any of the parties involved. It is easier to make unemotional decisions about sensitive money matters and use solid judgment when grieving is not clouding your thoughts.

Ideally both spouses are regularly involved with the family's finances. However, sometimes the responsibility is slanted toward one spouse more than another (or child who serves as the power of attorney for both parents). The information in the following section is most appropriate for the spouse or children with less experience.

Your relationship with your financial consultant could span decades!

Avoiding bad financial decisions is arguably more important than making good decisions. Hiring a less than ideal financial consultant will likely increase the number of bad financial decisions presented to you, so take the time to find a good one. The most stellar financial advisors tend to share three critical characteristics: integrity, compassion, and wisdom.

Integrity is a difficult characteristic to identify. If someone says "trust me," the natural inclination is the exact opposite. A reasonable way to screen for integrity is to talk to friends and relatives about their financial consultants: ask if they trust them and why. This dialogue will allow a little insight into the personality and integrity of the advisor you are considering hiring.

Integrity is more easily identified in an individual over the passage of time. When someone tells you something that is proven true or events occur as that person stated, a foundation of trust is built in that relationship. That doesn't mean mistakes won't happen. Everyone makes mistakes. When a financial consultant errs, the honesty and punctuality with which he or she responds to the situation speaks volumes about character.

Regulatory organizations monitor the services of the professionals you are interviewing and may offer some insight. Ask consultants how their profession is regulated and how you can contact their consumer protection services. Keep in mind that a complaint filed with the regulatory agency does not indicate an individual is a bad candidate. However, multiple complaints should raise a red flag.

Tip: In the investment brokerage arena, one regulatory body is the National Association of Securities Dealers Regulatory (NASDR), which offers information about every licensed investment broker. Go to "NASD BrokerCheck" at *www.NASD.com* for details. For financial planners, consider talking to your trusted friends or a family attorney for recommendations. A list of practical interview questions to ask a planner can be found at the Certified Financial Planner Board of Standards site: *www.cfp.net/Learn/knowledgebase.asp?id=8*

As you interview your potential financial consultant, don't be afraid to ask questions to help gauge integrity. Here are some examples of interview icebreakers that often offer a window to the consultant's soul. There are no pat answers to such questions and answering them on the spot requires a certain amount of honesty and frankness.

- Tell me what motivated you to pursue a career in financial services.

- What are the most gratifying aspects of your career?

- What is the biggest mistake you have made in your career?

- How did you handle your biggest mistake?

- What is the greatest success of your career?

- What do you value most about your life?

Although integrity is difficult to gauge in a brief interview, if you sense the professional passed the integrity test, ask for a few references to further investigate. Be sure to follow up with the references.

In the relationship you are essentially the advisor's employer. Although the advisor may seem to have a professional presence that implies he or she is in charge, you have complete authority to remove that person from his or her role at any time. So don't be intimidated or timid. Ask questions and voice any concerns you might have. The relationship is a two-way street, and its success over the long run requires open and honest communication.

Having said this, open and honest conversation can involve conflict, but this doesn't mean the relationship is not strong or that your financial consultant's advice isn't viable. When dealing with money and markets, emotions can make it difficult to remain objective and consequently discussions can sometimes become passionate. This is normal.

Compassion is the ability to understand and appreciate a situation and is critical for sustaining a good working relationship, particularly when you are dealing with major life changes. For example, reflect over the last five years of your life. What events occurred during those years that you did not anticipate? Are there some positive events? How about any negative occurrences? Had you been working

Ask candid questions.

You are the employer.

with a financial consultant, would the impact of these events have been the same?

Compassion is an attribute that is difficult to gauge in a brief engagement, but there are subtle indicators such as body language, voice tone, and listening skills that offer insight. It is difficult to have great compassion for people without knowing them but the empathy offered by a financial consultant is a critical element in the selection process and should be considered.

Wisdom is a nonnegotiable requirement. It is the ability to combine your situation and the economy with available financial tools to logically transform financial goals and challenges into understandable solutions and strategies.

Wisdom is significantly different from knowledge. Knowledge is simply a general awareness of facts, ideas, and principles, whereas wisdom is the judicious application of this information. A knowledgeable person may know a lot of words but a wise person is like a skilled writer who translates that vocabulary into a world-class novel. Frequently, individuals who don't really have wisdom try to mimic wisdom with their knowledge.

A good way to test a consultant's wisdom is to ask him or her to explain a financial concept in layman's terms. For example, "beta" in the financial industry is defined as "a measure of the volatility, or systemic risk, of a security or a portfolio in comparison to the market as a whole."[2] A wise consultant might define this term to you as "the risk of a particular investment in comparison with the risk of the market in general." The skilled consultant wants the client to understand the concept or reality being discussed. He or she does not want you to be impressed or bewildered by professional lingo. And he or she certainly doesn't want clients to feel embarrassed and stupid. The consultant should be able to explain financial concepts in a way that any adult can grasp.

There are certain components of disclosure that are required by law. Unfortunately, not everything required by law is easy to understand. There are certain investments that are sold by a prospectus. A prospectus is a legal document that explains risks, costs, and a variety of

---

[2] Investopedia, http://investopedia.com (accessed May 25, 2007).

other bits of information that the average investor would find difficult to understand.

Your ideal advisor will be able to explain the intricacies of your plan, but will likely only explain the basic workings of your plan and not every minute detail. If your personality requires such detailed information, be sure to point this out early in the process. Some individuals are happy to elaborate, and others prefer not to do so. Neither personality style nor preference indicates a character flaw one way or the other. It is simply a difference in innate personalities and communication styles. Just make sure that the demands of your personality are a good match with those the financial advisor exhibits.

If you can find a person with the knowledge of the financial services industry who also has the characteristics of wisdom, integrity, and compassion, and the ability to tie all of the necessary critical analyses into succinct understandable conversations, you are very fortunate. If you find such a consultant, that person is worth his or her weight in gold.

How Your Advisor Is Compensated

Once you find a suitable financial advisor, make sure you understand how he or she is compensated for services. In today's market financial advisors are generally compensated 1 percent annually for the assets they manage.

This 1 percent figure is a practical benchmark to consider. Generally, the larger the sum of money handled by the consultant, the lower the fee might be. This discussion is another good indicator of the character of the consultant. When asked, a seasoned consultant will generally be open and clear about how he or she is compensated.

The Financial Advisor Questionnaire (next page) has a list of additional questions to consider in your interview process beyond the suggestions included in this chapter. Your financial future is at stake; don't be bashful when it comes to interviewing your potential financial consultant!

Once you have hired your financial consultant, keep in mind the importance of continued communication. Call him or her with your questions and concerns. Depending on the type of question, the consultant will either quickly answer you or have the appropriate person on the consulting team respond.

Make sure your advisor knows about significant changes in your life. There are often strategies the advisor can implement to help you during changing life stages. Also, if you have expectations about the frequency of your communication with your consultant, make sure he or she is aware of those expectations. The more your advisor knows about you, your situation, and your preferences, the better he or she can serve you.

It is reasonable to consolidate your investment assets with one financial consultant. Some might think this is not appropriate diversification, but a high-caliber consultant should offer plenty of diversification of your assets.

There are several benefits of consolidating your investments with a single advisor. Many advisors allocate their time based on the amount of assets families have entrusted to them. Consequently, the more you have with one advisor, the more attention that advisor will be able to provide you. Not only will the advisor have more time available, but he or she will also have a better understanding of your overall situation. This consolidation process can help save your loved ones time. I am such a believer in this idea that I have suggested clients with significant wealth move the assets they have with me to another institution to better serve their family. This is not an everyday effort of mine, but I genuinely believe it is best for everyone.

> **Keep your financial consultant up to date about critical life changes.**

Financial Advisor Questionnaire

- How long have you been in the business?
- How long are you planning to be in the business?
- What does retirement look like for you?
- What type of experience and educational background do you have?
- What type of licensing/registration do you have?
- Briefly describe your investment philosophy.

- What area of planning is your specialty?

- How will you monitor my account?

- How often will we meet to review my account?

- Do you have minimum account sizes you work with and will I qualify to meet that standard for the foreseeable future?

- Can you provide references of clients who are in a situation similar to mine?

- What happens to my account if something happens to you?

- Who will help me if you are not available?

- Exactly how do I pay you?

- Which estate planning attorneys and accountants would you refer me to?

You and your heirs will normally need to talk with numerous other advisors and entities, each with their own buzzwords and industry procedures. Some of them may not be accustomed to communicating with grieving individuals. These may include:

- Financial advisors
- Bankers
- Life insurance representatives
- Property and casualty agents
- Estate planning attorneys
- Accountants
- Utilities
- Credit card companies
- Investment companies

It is helpful to bring a friend or relative to meetings to provide an extra set of ears, ask appropriate questions, take notes, and provide support and backup memory after the meeting during the grieving time. Keeping a journal will also ensure some record of the most pertinent information during your conversations. You can also use a microcassette player to record important discussions.

Your financial advisor should be willing to serve as your quarterback in communicating with these entities. It is important for your heirs to meet with your financial consultant early on when they are cleaning up your finances; this will allow them to determine how much the consultant is willing and able to help.

Be patient during this estate settlement process. It will get done, but it may take extra time. Many organizations have large service centers and a transient workforce, which sometimes increase the probability of clerical mistakes or misinformation. Some processes may not be completed on the first or second try, but persistence and documentation helps accelerate the effort.

An Extra Set of Eyes

You have heard the saying "a picture is worth a thousand words." We process much of life through our eyes and not our ears. Visual indicators can help sort out what's going on around us as long as we are attuned to them.

For example, an overgrown yard in the summertime or an unplowed snowy driveway in the wintertime might indicate a neighbor is on vacation. A stack of disorganized papers on an attorney's desk might signify something about the attorney's administrative skills and give you an idea about the promptness with which he or she will administer an estate. A friendly, receptive assistant at an accountant's office might indicate his or her familiarity with your situation and his or her discernment in handling a grieving person with tender loving care.

These examples are somewhat intuitive and a function of your observation skills. *Although your heirs might generally have skills of observation and intuition, they might find themselves less able to access these extraordinary skills during the grieving process.*

A friend or family member who is gifted in the area of observation may provide a great benefit to your heirs during this time to:

- ensure they are not being taken advantage of by a supplier or advisor.

Designate a close friend or family member to join you in meetings.

- notice significant changes in their house, whether the changes are from neglect or simply involve normal problems that might escape their notice.

- observe behavioral changes your loved ones might transition through just before, during, or after a loss.

Consider giving this person a set of keys to your house. This will allow this person to check on your loved ones after a loss without having to call the fire department or other emergency service.

Caring individuals can be crucial advocates during your time of grief. However, survivors need to give their extra set of eyes the freedom to point out observations without constant fear of hurt feelings. If your heirs shut the extra set of eyes down, he or she might be hesitant to continue pointing out observations that are truly in their best interest.

Choose someone to keep an eye on you and your house to help identify unexplained changes.

If your loved ones' extra set of eyes is someone who is a family member, you need to consider that person's counsel very seriously. If he or she is not a family member, you need to give him or her the authority to speak to an appropriate family member about observations so that someone with the necessary influence can intervene—if necessary. Think about this now and hold open discussions about these issues with those you love before you lose them.

Professionals Can Help Significantly

There are a number of professionals your loved ones may need to interact with as they sort through your estate. It is wise to have one as the focal point or leader. Your financial consultant may be ideal in that leadership role.

Your financial advisor's background should allow him to act as your quarterback.

The Certified Financial Planner® designation is part of my basis for suggesting that the financial consultant lead the way among the professionals. The CFP® designation requires significant training in tax, legal, investment, retirement, and insurance issues. If your financial consultant has earned the CFP® designation, he or she speaks the language of most of the other professionals you will need to work with following a loss in the family.

Even if the financial consultant doesn't hold the CFP® designation, he or she may still be a good selection as your leader. The pure competition in the marketplace has forced financial consultants to gain a deeper knowledge of the entire financial planning process—with or without the official Certified Financial Planner® designation. See the Key Advisors Directory provided at the end of this chapter. Make sure this is filled out and copies are provided to your attorney, financial planner, and loved ones.

Three other professionals who may become important in the days ahead include your accountant, attorney, and insurance agent. They all can help simplify your heirs' lives. Occasionally you will hear conflicting recommendations from your advisors. The conflict does not necessarily mean one is wrong, but instead may be just a reflection of that consultant's particular philosophy of the planning process.

Occasionally your advisors will have differing points of view.

For example, I believe debt-free living leads to a more peaceful lifestyle and a better overall financial plan. Some accountants argue that their clients would do well to keep a mortgage because they can deduct mortgage interest from their taxes. Even so, my opinion does not neglect the economics of the situation. If you pay a dollar in interest and you are in the 25 percent tax bracket, the dollar saved you twenty-five cents. If your mortgage were eliminated you would have to pay the twenty-five cents in taxes, but you would save the other seventy-five cents in interest. There are many other areas where different professionals will follow different methods to try to get to the same place.

Your accountant will be able to help consider the tax issues relative to your situation, not only today but also in the months ahead. Accountants are not only helpful in crunching numbers and filing tax forms, but ideally they also are abreast of the current tax laws and can help your loved ones make the best decisions about their future and save them taxes.

Find an accountant who stays current with the latest tax laws.

Accountants are available with a variety of backgrounds and from various sizes of companies. Suggest to your heirs that they consider hiring an accountant who is younger than them to lower the likelihood the accountant will retire and have to be replaced. As possible accountants are interviewed, your heirs should ask about their backgrounds, experience, and ambition to keep up to date with changes in the tax code. Past experience is important, but the ability to stay current is also critical. Tax laws change frequently and require accountants to keep up with their continuing education.

Your heirs' attorney will help in three distinct areas in the near term. He or she can help intervene in business issues if you own a business, he or she can close the estate, and he or she can advise your loved ones in updating their estate plans. An estate planning attorney can also help strategize the best ways to position assets to minimize unnecessary death taxes.

Like accountants, it is important for attorneys to stay abreast of changes in their field as the estate laws are constantly changing. Those changes often make it imperative to update your legal documents. Because it is likely you will spend time with your attorney on an ongoing basis, be sure you are comfortable with his or her personality. Your financial consultant probably works with a number of attorneys and can refer you to one who may be a good fit with your situation and personality.

Often a family's life insurance agent is separate from their property and casualty agent; either way, both areas will need some review and input in the months surrounding a death. Usually when there are insurance proceeds, the insurance company deposits the lump sum in a money market account at the company and provides your heirs with a checkbook to make withdrawals as necessary. This liquidity, or availability of assets, may prove to be very helpful in the near term.

You may have existing relationships with all of these advisors, or you may need referrals to the appropriate experts. Your financial consultant likely has experts in each area whom he or she trusts and is willing to refer. These referrals should save you a great deal of time and should provide you with high-caliber individuals. If one professional refers you to another, that professional's own reputation is on the line and it is not likely he or she would risk it for a mediocre relationship.

Also, if you have existing relationships that you believe will continue to offer value to your heirs, be sure to introduce the parties to one another before they will ever need to meet on a reactive basis. This will help smooth out the transition for your loved ones.

> Addressing business continuation, closure of the estate, and updating documents are three normal activities for your attorney.

> Your insurance agents will need to update your coverage and help add liquidity.

One widow made a remarkable comment about her husband's ability to address many of these needs in advance. "He wasn't a very demonstrative man. But I really know how much he loved me by having such specific instructions in place along with the professional relationships that were already in place."

Preferably, all of your critical relationships are already in place!

Key Advisors Directory

Financial Consultant: _____
    Address: _____
    Phone(s): _____

Attorney: _____
    Address: _____
    Phone(s): _____

Account/Tax Advisor: _____
    Address: _____
    Phone(s): _____

Life Insurance Agent: _____
    Address: _____
    Phone(s): _____

Property/Casualty Insurance Agent: _____
    Address: _____
    Phone(s): _____

Bank: _____
    Local Manager: _____
    Address: _____
    Phone(s): _____

Other: _____
    Address: _____
    Phone(s): _____

Other: _____
    Address: _____
    Phone(s): _____

What Now?

The loss of a spouse, parent, or another loved one is difficult. Making arrangements in advance softens the blow. The forms at the end of this chapter are designed to make this process easier and include a step-by-step plan for making funeral arrangements.

But what if you've already suffered the loss of a spouse, parent, or another loved one? As you know, it can be devastating. This guide, even after the fact, can be helpful. Like a tsunami, emotions can overcome survivors, making it difficult to prioritize important decisions and coordinate necessary activities immediately after a loved one's passing. Below is an outline of steps that can help streamline the process and offer some peace of mind.

The Death of a Loved One:
A Plan of Action

1. Day of Passing

a. Let the employees at the hospital/nursing home/hospice where your loved one died know which funeral home you have chosen to help with the final arrangements.

b. Ask loved ones to help communicate the loss to your inner circle of friends and family, reducing the number of phone calls required by you.

2. Second Day

a. Meet with the consultant at the funeral home to make the final arrangements.
   i. Check your safe-deposit box, in-home safe, and other places where valuable documents are stored to see if any details pertaining to final arrangements were previously outlined
   ii. Set times that are reasonable for you; most visitors to the funeral home will rearrange their schedule to accommodate yours.
   iii. Request two more death certificates than you think you need, just in case.

b. Try to enjoy the time with your family and loved ones.

c. Make arrangements to have specific family members and/or friends assigned to help with:
   i. Funeral arrangements
   ii. Reviewing and/or signing necessary financial/legal documents
   iii. A post-funeral meeting place

3. Funeral Day

a. Reflect on the fond memories of your loved one.

b. Secure a place that is quiet and private to retreat to if you need time away alone after the funeral.

4. One Week Later

a. Notify your financial institutions about the passing of your loved one. (Verify that there are enough liquid assets for the short term.)

b. Call your attorney to initiate legal work.

c. Call Social Security, your loved one's former employer, credit card companies, and any other entity that might need to know about the death.

5. Two Weeks to One Month Later

a. Meet with your financial advisor and other financial institutions to complete necessary paperwork.

b. Meet with your attorney to begin the necessary paperwork and to update your estate documents with new beneficiaries and other changes.

c. Complete the necessary paper work from Social Security, credit cards, and former employers.
   i. Your financial advisor might be a good source to review these documents on your behalf.
   ii. Some credit cards have life insurance included; check with them before you pay the final invoice; some may forgive debt depending on the situation.

Most financial institutions will work with you through this difficult time to make the process as easy as possible. Consider bringing a family member to your meetings to allow you an extra set of ears to listen to the instructions you will be receiving.

Don't feel compelled to make immediate decisions. You will likely make some critical decisions during this transition, but the grieving process can make it difficult to make the *best* decisions. Don't feel embarrassed about moving slowly; ask people to repeat themselves, and get second opinions. One widow told me it took her five years to begin thinking clearly again. There is a greater likelihood of making the best decisions after advisors (financial consultants, attorneys, bankers, accountants, insurance representatives, etc.) have been consulted.

Your financial consultant has likely helped other families through difficult times and can offer insight in a variety of areas. Don't be afraid to ask him or her for help regardless of the topic. The advisor is there for you!

Take your time with important decisions, and seek advice.

Journaling

The Loss of a Loved One Can Generate a Flood of Thoughts

When the unexpected call announcing my father's death came, it was staggering how many thoughts filled my mind within seconds of the news. My immediate response was to take a shower and try to organize my thoughts so as to respond appropriately. For whatever reason, the shower tends to be my think tank. It's my way of "taking every thought captive," as the Bible suggests in 2 Corinthians 10:5.

It is important to process our thoughts before we respond to them, particularly during a time of intense emotional pressure. There are many techniques that help people sort through their thoughts. Journaling is one such technique that many people find helpful.

Journaling is an exercise that can help you get your thoughts out of your head and onto paper where you can organize them in a logical manner. It is a great system for dealing with important decisions, especially when those decisions come at a moment when we can't give them our full attention. The thoughts accompanying a loss often cloud our minds, making it easy to neglect (or forget) an important decision or to record an essential thought about the lost loved one.

During my early years in business, often the solution to a problem I was wrestling with would pop into my mind in the middle of the night. Instead of carrying this thought in my head all night, I would call my voicemail and record the thought so that I could then relax the remainder of the night and go back to sleep.

Journaling allows us to clear our minds of the thoughts that clutter them. These thoughts, which need to be preserved, may include to-dos, strategies, promises, memories, and frustrations we feel when someone we love passes away. By writing the thoughts down, they won't be lost. We can leave tomorrow's issues for tomorrow, confident that when tomorrow comes, those thoughts will be there, recorded in the journal.

Your journal can be as simple as a spiral notebook or something more formal. Some of the notes may only be necessary until particular processes are completed; but others, like your fond memories, you will want to keep and reflect on from time to time.

Journaling can reduce stress and mistakes.

Journaling conversations you have with key people can also help you keep track of actions you need to take, giving you a clear record of what you've done and what you still need to do. An added benefit to journaling is that other individuals who are working with you or assisting you are more likely to pay attention to your issues if they perceive that you are paying careful attention to them. Conscientiousness is contagious. Some significant conversations to journal are:

- Financial consultant conversations

- Attorney conversations

- Employer benefit conversations

- Social Security Administration conversations

- Funeral home conversations

- Insurance company conversations

- Fond memories of your loved one

- Special gestures of kindness from friends, business acquaintances, family, neighbors

- Thoughts and concerns to process for extended family

- Letters, conversations, and prayers with God

My Funeral/Burial Instructions

Arrangements for:

_____

1. Services location:

(Church / Funeral Chapel / Cemetery / Other / None)

Church: _____ Phone: _____

Pastor: _____ Phone: _____

Funeral Home: _____ Phone: _____

Cemetery: _____ Phone: _____

Other: _____ Phone: _____

2. Funeral Preferences:

Funeral Certificate # _____

Visitation: (Family and Friends / Immediate Family Only / None)

Times for Visitation: _____

Casket Preference: _____

Clothing: _____

Military Service: (Yes / No) Flag: (Yes / No)

Transportation: Lead Car: (Yes / No)   Clergy Car: (Yes / No)   Family Limo: (Yes / No)

Pallbearers:

_____   _____

_____   _____

_____   _____

_____   _____

3. Burial Preference:

Certificate of Burial Rights # _____

Type: (Ground Burial / Mausoleum / Cremation or Memorialization / Other)

Certificate in Name of: _____

In-Ground Interment: Section _____ Lot _____ Block _____ Grave _____

Vault Preference: _____

Above Ground Entombment: Section _____ Row _____ Level _____ Crypt # _____

Columbarium: Section _____ Row _____ Level _____ Niche # _____

4. Memorialization Preferences:

Type: (Flush Memorial / Upright Memorial / Companion / Single / Other)

    (Granite / Bronze / Urn)

5. Personal Preferences:

Flowers and Memorial Gifts:

___ Flowers

___ Either Flowers or Memorial Contributions

___ Prefer Memorial Contributions Made to: _____

Glasses to Be Worn? ____ Yes ___ No

Jewelry: ____ Stay on ___ Return to: _____

Musicians: _____

Music Selections: _____

Scriptural References: _____

Personal Requests and Wishes: _____

Relatives and Friends to Be Notified

(Highlight those who can be of immediate assistance)

Children:

	Phone/Cell: _____
_____	Phone/Cell: _____
_____	Phone/Cell: _____
_____	Phone/Cell: _____
_____	Phone/Cell: _____
_____	Phone/Cell: _____

Parents:

	Phone/Cell: _____
_____	Phone/Cell: _____

Siblings:

	Phone/Cell: _____
_____	Phone/Cell: _____
_____	Phone/Cell: _____
_____	Phone/Cell: _____
_____	Phone/Cell: _____

Grandchildren _____ # Great Grandchildren _____ # Nieces _____ # Nephews _____

Other Friends and Relatives:

	Phone/Cell: _____
_____	Phone/Cell: _____
_____	Phone/Cell: _____
_____	Phone/Cell: _____
_____	Phone/Cell: _____
_____	Phone/Cell: _____

Personal Record

This information is necessary for a death certificate in many states. It will also be a helpful source for drafting an obituary.

Name _____

Address _____ Since _____

Previous Address _____ Since _____

State/Residence Since _____ County/Residence Since _____

Place of Birth _____

Birth date _____ U.S. Citizen (Yes / No) Naturalization # _____

Social Security # _____

Marital Status (Single / Married / Divorced / Widowed)

Name of Spouse _____ Anniversary _____

Children's Names _____

_____

Grandchildren's Names _____

_____

Great Grandchildren's Names _____

_____

Occupation _____ Employer _____ Since _____

Education/School _____ Degree _____ Year _____

Church/Clubs _____

Military Service _____

Father's Name _____ Place of birth _____

Mother's Name (maiden) _____ Place of birth _____

Special Recognitions and Achievements _____

_____

Special Background Interests _____

_____

Lifelong Passions _____

_____

GIVE THE GIFT OF

Financial Survivors
A Guide for Living Before Loss
TO YOUR FRIENDS AND FAMILY

CHECK YOUR LEADING BOOKSTORE OR ORDER HERE

❏ **YES**, I want _____ copies of *Financial Survivors* at $19.95 each, plus $4.95 shipping per book (Texas residents please add $1.65 sales tax per book). Canadian orders must be accompanied by a postal money order in U.S. funds. Allow 15 days for delivery.

❏ **YES**, I am interested in having Keith A. Tyner speak or give a seminar to my company, association, school, or organization. Please send information.

My check or money order for $_____ is enclosed.

Please charge my: ❏ Visa ❏ MasterCard ❏ Discover ❏ American Express

Name _____

Organization _____

Address _____

City/State/Zip _____

Phone_____ Email _____

Card # _____

Exp. Date_____ Signature _____

Please make your check payable and return to:

CEO IQ Publishing
2625 Main Street • Dallas, TX 75226

Call your credit card order to: (888) 826-6789
Fax: (214) 760-9715   www.ceoiq.com